Anthony Hopkins'
Snowdonia

First published in Great Britain in 1993 by
Colin Baxter Photography Ltd
Grantown-on-Spey
Morayshire, PH26 3NA
Scotland

First Published in Paperback in 1995

Photographs copyright © Graham Nobles 1993
Text copyright © Colin Baxter Photography Ltd 1993
Reprinted 1993
Reprinted 1994

The following poems are printed with the kind permission of their authors,
translators and publishers:

"Cynefin", page 11 by T. H. Parry-Williams, translated by Ioan Bowen Rees, Gomer Press.
"Y Daith", page 29 by Bryn ap Gwilym.
"Y Ci Defaid", page 49 by Thomas Richards, translated by Margaret Bowen Rees, Marian Elias.
"Bygythiad", page 65 by Dinah Griffiths.
"Dymuniad", page 85 by Nesta Wyn Jones, translated by Ioan Bowen Rees, Gomer Press.

British Library Cataloguing in Publication Data
Hopkins, Anthony
Anthony Hopkins' Snowdonia
I. Title
914.292504

ISBN 0-948661-45-3

Design by Zoë Hall, Studio Z, Edinburgh
Printed in Singapore

Front Cover Photograph: *Llyn Llydaw, Crib Goch and Snowdon under morning cloud.*

Anthony Hopkins'
Snowdonia

Photographs by Graham Nobles

Text by Bryn Havord

Captions by Anthony Hopkins

Colin Baxter Photography, Grantown-on-Spey, Scotland

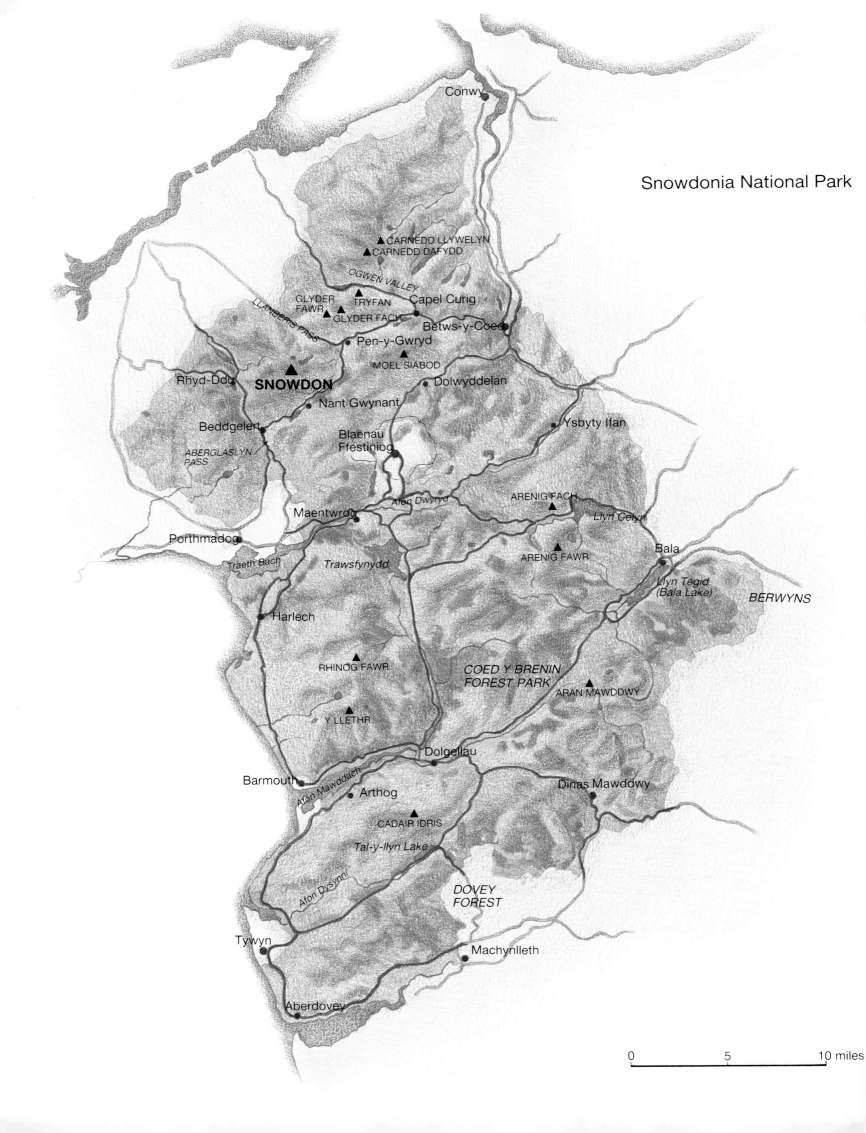

Snowdonia National Park

Conwy

CARNEDD LLYWELYN
CARNEDD DAFYDD

OGWEN VALLEY

GLYDER
FAWR
TRYFAN
GLYDER FACH
Capel Curig
LLANBERIS PASS
Betws-y-Coed
Pen-y-Gwryd
MOEL SIABOD

Rhyd-Ddu
SNOWDON
Dolwyddelan

Nant Gwynant
Ysbyty Ifan

Beddgelert
Blaenau
Ffestiniog

ABERGLASLYN
PASS
ARENIG FACH

Afon Dwyryd
Llyn Celyn

Maentwrog
ARENIG FAWR
Bala

Porthmadog
Llyn Tegid
(Bala Lake)
BERWYNS

Traeth Bach
Trawsfynydd

Harlech
RHINOG FAWR
COED Y BRENIN
FOREST PARK

ARAN MAWDDWY

Y LLETHR

Dolgellau
Dinas Mawddwy

Barmouth
Afon Mawddach
Arthog

CADAIR IDRIS

Tal-y-llyn Lake

Afon Dysynni
DOVEY
FOREST

Tywyn
Machynlleth

Aberdovey

0   5   10 miles

Contents

Foreword

It is always a joy to come home. Like many Welsh people I feel a distinct sense of *hiraeth* – which roughly translates to mean a deep longing or yearning. While I am fortunate enough to travel the world in the course of my work, there has always been a part of me that longs to be back in Wales, whether it be my native Port Talbot or the rugged countryside of North Wales. I feel a need to identify and experience a sense of harmony with the basic life force of Wales and its nature.

That is why I was honoured and pleased to become President of the National Trust Snowdonia Appeal. Snowdonia is one of the very few places left in Britain today where one can enjoy the wind-swept grandeur of the oldest of mountains, and just a step or two away, experience the intimate stillness of an oak wood, broken only by the sound of bird song or the tumble of a waterfall. This is a place to replenish the human spirit. It is precisely because such places are so rare in our modern world, that we must fight to prevent their destruction.

I have promised the National Trust that I will be no mere celebrity figurehead or photograph on a leaflet – that I am prepared to get my hands dirty too, by joining the hundreds of other volunteers who come to work in Snowdonia each year. I have recently been able to do just that – an exhausting and exhilarating time – doing some dry-stone walling. The sheer antiquity of the place seems to seep through your fingertips, as one lichen-covered rock is placed carefully against another.

But this is not just a piece of beautiful countryside. It is also a living and working environment for a network of small rural communities that bind Snowdonia together. This rare combination of landscape, wildlife habitat, community, culture and language is unparalleled anywhere else in Britain today. It is the sole-surviving part of a Britain long-since disappeared.

The National Trust owns and cares for around 50,000 acres of the most beautiful landscape in Snowdonia. That protection, on behalf of the nation – for all the people, for all time – is an important guarantee that future generations may also enjoy the solitude of an oak wood, the spectacle of butterflies over an orchid-filled meadow, or the view from one of Snowdonia's sentinel mountains.

Yet this superb landscape with its unique identity, is all at risk. I have seen for myself – from a bird's eye view in a helicopter – the encroaching ranks of conifer plantations, the dereliction of medieval dry-stone walls and the terrible erosion scars of over-visited mountainsides.

Crib y Ddysgl.

7

Snowdonia is under threat, but the positive work of the National Trust countryside workers, supported financially by thousands of Snowdonia well-wishers, gives hope for the future. It is an education to meet a member of a footpath repair team, whose work will last a hundred years, or a Warden who is supervising the natural regeneration of an ancient oak woodland – who knows that the fruit of his labours will reach maturity in 400 year's time. It is a humbling experience made more profound with a sense *cynefin* – the concept that this piece of land should be interpreted as if all the memories and actions of those who have ever lived there, are present today.

All this hard work – on our behalf and for future generations – has to be carefully managed and planned. It also must be paid for. As a charity, the National Trust relies on the generosity of thousands of individuals to the Snowdonia Appeal to finance its endeavours. The Appeal has already raised £800,000 since its launch at the end of 1990. But it needs over another £1 million before the end of 1995. This hard cash helps pay for a four man repair team which costs £40,000 per year, or a programme of dry-stone wall rehabilitation which costs £25,000 per year, or helps with the traditional organic management of wildflower meadows costing some £1,300 a year – and much, much more.

The photographs in this book provide a celebration of Snowdonia. Its purchase provides another contribution to the vital work programmes of the National Trust, be it the re-roofing of a traditional barn or for tools for a band of inner-city volunteers clearing rhododendrons, the provision of a haven for otters or the planting of an oak wood. This book will, I hope, help us to keep Snowdonia alive.

Snowdonia is a place full of magic. It would be a catastrophe to see it spoilt forever. So please join me in this mission. Become a National Trust Friend of Snowdonia. Together we can save Snowdonia. If you will help, please turn to the back of this book to see how you can make a difference.

Anthony Hopkins

In the Ogwen Valley, below Tryfan's classic profile.

Cynefin

I don't know who I am
On rich lowland lacking peat

– Down the centuries my red blood
has sensed the difference between land and land

But I know who I am, if given a hill
Peat-bog and rushes, rock and lake.

T. H. Parry-Williams

North Wales is a land of mountains and lakes, of granite and slate, of old hill farms and cascading rivers. There are castles, hill forts, stately homes, old mills, and wild mountain passes where armies have clashed down the ages. It is a land where the last independent Welsh princes held out for years against the English, and where bards and musicians sang of an ancient culture.

It is a region of haunting beauty and grandeur, of rocky mountains, hidden valleys, still glacial lakes, and deep forests. It is an old country: geologically old, with some of the most ancient rocks in the world; old in an economy still largely based on the sheep-rearing way of life; old in culture, with traditions in poetry and music that may date back to the Bronze Age and old in language, for the Welsh which is still spoken there is Europe's oldest living language. It is an area where the mountain recesses and the deep valleys seem to hold the echo of history, and the myths, legends and bardic traditions of the past. And within it, in the old kingdom of Gwynedd, is the jewel in the crown, known in Welsh as *Eryri* and in English as Snowdonia.

Its breathtaking, massive and brooding landscape was originally formed by intense volcanic activity, and finally sculpted into its present form by the great Ice Age more than 10,000 years ago. The recorded history of the area starts 2,000 years before the birth of Christ with the Bronze Age people, who left a legacy of great burial chambers, and stone circles such as Bryn Cader Faner which stands high in the hills above Harlech. The Iron Age brought Celtic tribesmen with their Druidic religious cult, and a language which was the precursor of modern Welsh.

When the Romans invaded the area and settled themselves at Segontium on the south western end of the Menai Strait, where the town of Caernarfon now stands, they found a people who could not be subjugated in the same way as the lowland tribes of England, and there followed a period which can only be described as an uneasy co-existence. After the Romans' departure,

Y Garn.

11

Moel Siabod sits squarely in splendid isolation, content in its own company.

the indigenous population retained some of their technical advances and an early form of Christianity. This they blended with what they remembered of the ideas and beliefs of the Druids and the Celtic animists, who believed that God lives in all natural things. It is that potent mixture of feeling and beliefs which has influenced Welsh thinking up to the present day, and which has been a powerful factor in the moulding of the Welsh character.

The Welsh word *cynefin*, which is much used in the sheep farming communities of Snowdonia, and which, in common with many other Welsh words, defies a direct translation into English, has a central sense of habitat or one's accustomed place, but it also refers to the unchanging strength of the countryside; the power of a tradition and the character of a people, the steadfastness of the community and the people within it, and it is undoubtedly this steadfastness which has helped the Welsh to not only retain, but develop, their identity throughout the Roman and subsequent invasions.

After the Romans there were skirmishes with the Irish, the Scots and the Vikings, and attacks from the Saxons in the east who by the 8th century controlled the land of the Britons which thus became Angle-land, or England. Offa, the Saxon king of Mercia, had a massive earthwork erected along its western border to keep out the Welsh, who by then were calling themselves the *Cymru*, or fellow countrymen. They retained their own language, the medium for their oral literature and their heroic tales, and maintained their tribal groupings, making a life for themselves in a mountainous environment which imposed its own stern disciplines.

Throughout the Dark Ages they developed their cultural and linguistic identity, as well as patterns of agriculture and methods of animal husbandry in harmony with the harsh environment. In the first half of the 12th century,

The stout keep of Castell Dolwyddelan stands sentinel to the upper reaches of the Afon Lledr.

Tryfan shrouded in mist, greets an unpromising dawn.

during the reign of Henry I, the Normans built a network of castles and established Marcher lordships which kept the Welsh in a vice-like grip. Over the next hundred years the English had troubles elsewhere, and taking advantage of the respite this gave Wales, the Welsh were able to develop their culture as never before.

Their language had been in continuous literary use since the 6th century, and in this period of peace they enjoyed a time of cultural renaissance and artistry which established them as one of the most cultured nations of the times. For centuries, legends and folk tales had been handed down in an oral tradition, either as hearth-talk among families and small communities, or by the *cyfarwyddion* - itinerant storytellers who provided entertainment at the courts of the Welsh princes. The major cycle of legends were transcribed around the end of the 14th century and is known as *The Mabinogion*: a collection of ancient Celtic myths about divinity, rebirth and the underworld, which contains the earliest Arthurian story, interpretations of historical events and political satire. It is regarded as one of the masterpieces of medieval literature.

In the first half of the 13th century the Welsh benefited from the strong and unifying leadership of Llywelyn the Great. On his death in 1240 he was succeeded by a powerful dynasty which only came to an end in 1282 when Llywelyn the Last was killed in a chance encounter with English knights while trying to raise support for a campaign against Edward I. With the end of the Llywelyns North Wales was overrun by the English, and Edward built a network of massive castles which stretched from Harlech to Cricieth, Caernarfon, Beaumaris, Conwy, Rhuddlan and Flint, in an attempt to contain and control the Welsh tribes, and by 1301, Wales had its first English prince.

A hundred years later, one of the most sustained revolts against English

Afon Glaslyn at Pont Croesor.

15

The ruined homesteads that litter the high pastures of Snowdonia attest to a time when our ancestors endured an often harsh and hostile existence. These simple dwellings appear little more than manipulations of earth and stone, belying our notion of "idyll".

rule began on a hillside beside the road between Corwen and Llangollen. There, in September 1400, the rebels proclaimed Owain Glyndŵr as the rightful Prince of Wales, and for the next ten years he waged a series of skilful campaigns against the armies of Henry IV. He captured the castles at Aberystwyth, Harlech and Conwy and set up parliaments at Machynlleth and Harlech. In addition to his achievements in battle he planned universities and upheld the laws created by Hywel Dda, that were based on fairness, logic and common sense. The momentum of the campaign could not, however, be maintained, and Glyndŵr had to go into hiding. He rejected the pardon proffered by Henry V and was never captured. Legend has it that he evaded the pursuing English by wading across the Afon Glaslyn and hiding in a cave below Moel Hebog, where he was fed and protected by the people of Beddgelert and the monks at a priory nearby. His fellow countrymen were devastated at the failure of the rebellion, but Glyndŵr had engendered in the Welsh a feeling of nationhood which survived the Acts of Union of 1536 and 1543, when Wales was absorbed into the United Kingdom of Great Britain, and which endures to this day.

Down the ages invaders and settlers have left artefacts and structural evidence of their periods of occupation and residency, but the megalithic circles and standing stones of the earliest peoples blend so well with their environment that they seem a part of it, and it often takes some time to realise that they were built to a design by human hands. The first man-made structures to have any real impact on the landscape were the Welsh castles such as Llywelyn the Great's Dolwyddelan and Dolbadarn, but they too strangely blended in with their surroundings. In contrast Edward's English castles were a high point in medieval military architecture, and are still referred to today by some as Edward's tax offices. Their psychological impact

A legacy of slate.

was massive, and although built with local stone, their alien bulk still dominates and imposes itself on the landscape.

With these castles, in a sense, the "disfigurement" of Snowdonia had begun, although the area has a long industrial history stretching back to the Romans who mined copper and lead, and some scars had already been left on the hills. But although a 15th century ode speaks of slates as "jewels from the hillside", farming remained the main occupation, supported by woollen and corn mills and localised crafts. Transport and communications were poor, which restricted expansion and movement, but even the remote area of Snowdonia could not forever remain aloof from the changes and demands resulting from the upsurge in industrialisation in the rest of Britain and the western world. From about 1750 onwards, entrepreneurs and local landowners became increasingly aware of the area's economic potential and began to exploit its rich resources.

Castell y Gwynt.

Slate quarrying had by far the largest impact at this time and developed rapidly from the end of the 18th century as the popularity of roofing slates increased, reaching its peak at the end of the 1890s. Slate is quarried using three basic methods: in the Nantlle Vale deep pits were excavated; at Blaenau Ffestiniog deep mining techniques were adopted; and around Bethesda and Llanberis the most visually intrusive method involving huge galleries, each about 60ft high, climbing and irrevocably scarring the mountain sides, was used. New methods of transportation had to be introduced to link the quarries with the main ports of Caernarfon, Porthmadog and Porth Dinorwig, and great feats of skill were demanded of the engineers who built the narrow-gauge railways which became the lifelines.

The methods of quarrying and mining the slate inflicted considerable visual damage on the area. Unfortunately producing useable slate is a very wasteful business, which has left the landscape with a legacy of huge tips of slate waste which still dominate parts of the sky-line. Some of the abandoned quarries have become flooded with rain-water which has completely transformed their appearance, and with their ruined buildings and sheer rock faces many of them are enjoying a new lease of life as sets for the film and advertising industries, but their value as part of our industrial heritage is increasingly being called into question.

A chain of stone quarries stretching from Chester to the Llŷn Peninsula was opened, and the granite rock above Penmaenmawr which had been worked in Neolithic times to produce axeheads, became popular in the 19th century for the production of stone setts, or cobblestones, used to build the roadways in the newly-industrialised towns in the north of England.

In 1852, 1862 and 1887 there were three separate gold rushes in the mountains to the north of Dolgellau which produced quite respectable amounts of the precious metal, and copper mining was carried out over a large area in the rest of Snowdonia, but unlike slate quarrying, this type of

Cadair Idris.

exploitation of the natural resources did little outward damage to the area, and the small mines on the mainland could not compare with those at Parys Mountain on Anglesey, where, in 1768, huge deposits of the ore were discovered.

North Wales was also particularly well-suited for iron manufacture, with its plentiful supplies of iron ore and large areas of coppice woodland for charcoal-making. It also had more than enough water to drive the waterwheels that were needed to power the bellows, so as early as 1597 a furnace was put in blast near Dolgellau, and by the middle of the 17th century there were a number of forges and furnaces at work in the area. One of the last to be built, in 1755, is in the aptly named village of Furnace, which lies a few miles to the south of Machynlleth, and is one of the best-preserved of its type.

Although apparently dominated by extractive industries, there was also a diversity of manufacturing industry in Snowdonia, and the knitting of stockings, usually done in the home, was widespread. It has been estimated that the annual sales of woollen products at Bala market in the 1790s were worth about £13,000, a very substantial amount when calculated in today's terms. With the abundance of water in the area the brewing of beer was popular, and at one time Bala was the home of the Welsh Whisky Works.

Until the end of the 18th century, the inhospitable terrain in Snowdonia made journeys both lengthy and hazardous, creating a serious impediment to the development of trade. Thomas Telford was therefore instructed to build "without regard to special interests" a road between Shrewsbury and Holyhead which was later to become the A5. In addition to the road, he also built the famous suspension bridge over the Menai Strait, which until recently, was the only road linking Anglesey to the mainland. As the canal network spread its tentacles into North Wales, Telford was also responsible for the construction of the massive aqueduct that carries the Llangollen Canal over the River Dee to the basin at Pont-Cysyllte, which is over 1,000ft long and stands 127ft above the valley.

The coming of the railways in the 19th century gave access to those parts of North Wales that had not benefited from the building of roads and canals. The main lines initially served the slate-producing areas, and subsequently, smaller branch lines began to break down the isolation of the more rural areas. The achievements of the railway-builders who met the challenges presented by the formidable countryside and enabled the first train to travel between Chester and Holyhead in 1850, were remarkable.

This was the Golden Age of the Grand Tour by the English aristocracy, whose travels in Europe and the near east were accompanied by their passion for collecting items of artistic value. With the access to Snowdonia opened up by the developments in the transport infrastructure to service the new industries, some of these wealthy travellers turned their attentions to North

The Pass of Llanberis is a begrudging thoroughfare. The narrow road stumbles from Pen y Pass to Nant Peris, forcing its way through rocky debris, gushing streams and hastily buttressed scree. Finally, it arrives at Llyn Padarn.

Crib y Ddysgl.

Wales, and the area witnessed the birth of another phenomenon: tourism.

Although Giraldus Cambrensis had made his epic journey through the country at the end of the 12th century, and has since been dubbed as Wales' first tourist, the purpose of his visit was to recruit soldiers for the Third Crusade, not to enjoy the landscape, and it was only with the beginning of the Romantic Era at the end of the 18th century that the grandeur of Snowdonia and its mountains began to be appreciated. Until then, the landscape had usually been looked upon in terms of its potential for productivity, sustenance and profit, with the mountains regarded as alien, sterile and barbarous. They were also viewed by many with suspicion and caution as the natural habitat of wild animals and bandits, and in Snowdonia, at Twll Du, it was said that the devil himself boiled up cloud and storms in his kitchen to threaten the lives of unsuspecting sailors.

Richard Wilson, a Welsh artist of genius, was the first painter to record the landscape of the area. In the 1760s he painted *Snowdon from Llyn Nantlle*, and in 1774, *Llyn-y-Cau, Cadair Idris,* and he is reputed to have said that everything the landscape-painter could want was to be found in North Wales. It certainly appealed to English artists like J. M. W. Turner who painted *Dolbadarn Castle* in 1798 and *Caernarfon Castle* in 1833, and to John Sell Cotman who painted *Snowdon* in 1809.

The early tourism, however, was the preserve of the rich and possibly the eccentric, and it was usually those with a definite purpose who ventured across Offa's Dyke to behold the newly discovered wonders: geologists

21

Y Lliwedd scatters the rays of sunlight, and forges the memory of a moment that will last a lifetime.

were keen to discover in detail how the mountains had been formed; ornithologists came to study the birdlife; horticulturists scanned the peatlands and crags for signs of rare species, and archaeologists arrived to study the material remains of the early cultures. The mountains had been climbed since early times as evidenced by the cairns on even the highest peaks, but it was only now that the question of climbing them for sport arose. The Napoleonic Wars had put the Alps out of bounds to English climbers, and the mountains of Snowdonia offered them an excellent alternative.

Climbs of considerable complexity and difficulty had certainly been made by some of the local men years before the English "alpinists" made their first recorded ascents, and the Slanting Gulley on Y Lliwedd had almost certainly been climbed in around 1850 by copper miners from Nant Gwynant, who were tempted by the legend of King Arthur's gold being hidden in a cave two-thirds of the way up, some forty years before the Abraham brothers from Keswick reached its top in 1897.

In Norfolk, on 27 July 1854, a massive dark-haired man named George Borrow bundled his wife Mary and his step-daughter Henrietta into a train. It was the start of a journey to North Wales where he began his epic walk through the country, which culminated in the publication of *Wild Wales* in 1862. The book was written in the rather patronising style of the times and it is not surprising, therefore, that it has never been popular with the Welsh. Neither was it an immediate success elsewhere, but it eventually became popular, probably as a result of the mounting interest in tourism in Wales

Pen yr Ole Wen.

22

24

rather than its literary merit, and it is constantly reprinted. The book has been subjected to a considerable amount of academic scrutiny and discussion. Nevertheless, if a true account, it gives a fascinating insight into the people, language and scenery of Snowdonia, and indeed the rest of Wales, in the middle of the 19th century.

The developing interest in travel and the countryside was not confined to North Wales. In the middle of the 19th century William Wordsworth wrote one of the earliest tourist guide-books *Guide to the Lakes*. In it he put forward his idea that the Lake District should become "a sort of national property, in which every man has a right and interest who has an eye to perceive and a heart to enjoy". Needless to say, the landowners did not welcome this suggestion with open arms, and continued to resist any attempts by the public to gain access to their property. The new breed of industrial workers were glad to escape to the countryside as a cheap form of relief from the restrictions and grinding conditions of their everyday lives, and, eventually, in the early 1930s, freedom of the hills became their campaign. In 1932, there was a mass trespass on Kinder Scout in the Peak District, and men were subsequently sent to prison for having the temerity to demand the right to walk in the countryside.

The pressure for the creation of National Parks was intensified by ramblers, country lovers and other enlightened thinkers and in 1936 the Standing Committee for National Parks was established to press the Government to introduce legislation. In their *Case for National Parks in Great Britain*, published in 1938, the historian G. M. Trevelyan wrote in the foreword, "The Government undertakes to assist the health of the nation and to find playing fields for the dwellers in the vast cities to play cricket and football. But it is no less essential, for any national health scheme, to

Cynefin is both a backyard and a country. An interlinking tapestry of time and place where men and women have worked and dreamed, celebrated and mourned, lived and died. And where land and wildlife form a backdrop to the sagas and tragedies of life. Capel Curig (left). Castell Dolbadarn (above).

preserve for the nation walking grounds and regions where young and old can enjoy the sight of unspoiled nature. And it is not a question of physical exercise only, it is also a question of spiritual exercise and enjoyment. It is a question of spiritual values. Without sight of the beauty of nature the spiritual power of the British people will be atrophied".

The Standing Committee further developed the discussion for the creation of National Parks when it said "Great Britain has a strictly limited amount of unspoilt wilder country and there are many encroachments upon it - not only for weekend cottages, new or improved motor roads, car parks, filling-stations, road-houses, advertisement hoardings and all the paraphernalia that meet the needs of the 'country lover', but also for such economic and public developments as water-catchment, electric power schemes, artillery and bombing grounds, mining, quarrying and commercial afforestation."

"There is not a square mile too much of wilder country, and there is urgent need of a national policy for conserving the whole."

The arguments gathered momentum and the various pressure groups started to establish themselves into formal organisations such as the Ramblers' Association, the Council for the Preservation of Rural England, the Friends of the Lake District and the Youth Hostels Association.

The campaign was interrupted by the Second World War, but in 1945, the idea of creating National Parks became an integral part of the plan for the reconstruction and rejuvenation of a Britain which had suffered deprivation and been battered by five years of warfare. John Dower, a civil servant and a leading member of the Standing Committee for National Parks produced the definitive report on how National Parks could become a reality. This was followed by the Hobhouse Report which illustrated how the Parks could be administered by local government, and in 1949, with the passing of the National Parks and Access to the Countryside Act, the dream of countless country lovers became a reality. In 1951 the Peak Park was the first National Park to be set up, followed in the same year by the Snowdonia National Park.

In common with the Welsh nation, the Snowdonia National Park has many facets, and consists of many different layers. It is a very complex organisation and the Snowdonia National Park Authority works closely with the National Trust, Gwynedd County Council, Cadw Welsh Historic Monuments, the Snowdonia National Park Society and many other organisations, as well as a huge army of volunteers and benefactors, who all work to conserve the environment for the benefit of all who live and work here, attempting to create an environment where visitors can relax and enjoy the countryside, and possibly experience for themselves the true meaning of *cynefin*.

Craig Lwyd overlooks the valley road from Minffordd to Corris.

Y Daith

When I travel wide to gaze on and broaden horizons,
I'm drawn by cords of steel, back to an ancient country,
to make a journey in the land of my fathers,
and quell the burning hiraeth, deep in my soul.

Bryn ap Gwilym

The Snowdonia National Park covers an area of 840 square miles and is the second largest, and some say the most spectacular, National Park in England and Wales. An estimated 12 million people visit it each year to climb the mountains, look at the wildlife, walk through the forests, laze on the beaches or simply drive around and look at the breathtaking scenery. The name Snowdonia is in fact a misnomer, which is probably the result of conquerors asking not "what is this place called?" but saying "what shall we call this place?" In Welsh it is *Eryri* – land of eagles, although these splendid predators haven't lived here for the last three hundred years. The summit of Snowdon itself is called *Yr Wyddfa* – burial mound, which is often mistakenly used as the name for the whole mountain.

From whichever direction it is approached: from Anglesey, where at Menai Bridge it is seen as one glorious panorama; from the Cambrian mountains of mid-Wales where it presents itself almost unannounced; through the gentle Clwydian hills, or along the most popular route from Betws y Coed, it is difficult to ignore a mounting sense of excitement and anticipation, and impossible to dispel the strange brooding atmosphere of the whole place, whatever the weather.

The most photographed and classic approach to Snowdon itself has to be from just outside Capel Curig, where at the Plas y Brenin National Mountain Centre the road turns south-westerly, and if it is a fine day, the Snowdon massif is mirrored in the twin surfaces of the Llynnau Mymbyr. A few miles further on, near the Pen-y-Gwryd Inn, a road turns sharply off to the right and leads to the top of the Llanberis Pass, where at Pen-y-Pass the awesome majesty of Snowdonia finally starts to reveal itself. Here the impressive peak of Crib Goch stands sentinel; it is the start of the Snowdon Horseshoe and one of the most dangerous and famous knife-edge ridges in Britain, often mistaken for Snowdon itself. And it is from here that the Pyg Track starts its winding path on through Bwlch y Moch with Carnedd Ugain, the summit of Crib y Ddysgl, high on the right, and with its views across Llyn Llydaw to the twin peaks of Y Lliwedd, and then on to Yr Wyddfa.

Llyn Gwynant and Moel Hebog.

It is easy in this atmospheric setting for susceptible visitors to be carried away by the poetry and magic of the Celtic myths and legends which were brewed up in the cauldron of Welsh nationhood, and this is the backdrop for one of the most famous stories. King Arthur's treacherous nephew Modred formed an alliance with the Saxons to overthrow the King, and their armies gathered in the hills. Arthur discovered the plan and marched to confront the rebels at Tregalan above Cwm y Llan. The ensuing battle was bloody, but Arthur slowly forced his enemies up the hillside to the pass between Yr Wyddfa and Y Lliwedd. In the winter dusk Arthur was hit by an arrow, but before he died he slew Modred with one mighty blow from his sword Excalibur. Sir Bedivere carried the King down to Llyn Llydaw where he was ferried away to the other world, and Arthur's few remaining

Crib Goch (left) looms ominously above Pen y Pass, while the notorious Pinnacles (right) guard the northern approach to the Snowdon Horseshoe.

The Snowdon range viewed across Llynnau Mymbyr, a classic Snowdonia set-piece.

knights withdrew to a cave hidden in Lliwedd's precipices where they fell into an enchanted slumber, waiting for their leader to return. Legend has it that there they still wait . . . and when Wales is under mortal threat, Arthur will awaken them, and together they will come to the nation's rescue. The place has since been known as *Bwlch y Saethau* – Pass of the Arrows.

The Llanberis Pass probably retains better than any other area the evidence of the maelstrom of volcanic and glacial activity which ravaged North Wales, and created the area's topography. It is a primeval, gaunt and uneasy place. There is the ubiquitous scree, huge boulders, bigger than the average sized house, crags, buttresses, tumbling streams of water which turn into raging torrents within minutes of rain falling on the peaks, and a few bleak and lonely farmhouses. The road makes its tortuous journey down from Pen y Pass, hemmed in by Snowdon on the one hand and The Glyders on the other, to the village of Nant Peris, and on past the ruins of Dolbadarn Castle to the old slate-quarrying village of Llanberis, just outside the Park border. In 1896, the Snowdon Mountain Railway was opened to carry the less intrepid visitors from Llanberis to the summit, but at the inaugural ceremony to launch the service its first Swiss-built locomotive was derailed, and to this day the company has never had a Locomotive No.1. Here the despoliation of the area is all too evident, with the huge galleries created by the slate quarrying industry dominating the scene to the north-east.

To the north, and also best approached from Capel Curig lie the Ogwen Valley and the Nant Ffrancon Pass, which are much broader and less claustrophobic than the Llanberis Pass, overshadowed on one side by Glyder

Clogwyn Du bright for once, before a brooding Crib Goch.

Fach, Tryfan and Y Garn, and on the other by Carnedd Dafydd, Carnedd Llywelyn and the Carneddau, the great northern range in the principality. In the north of the area the mountains are smooth-profiled and grassy, interspersed with the occasional rocky outcrop, but further south, nearer to the Ogwen Valley, are Ysgolion Duon – the Black Ladders, and Craig yr Isaf, two of the greatest cliffs in Wales. A popular, if strenuous walk starts at Garreg Fawr, a short time after leaving the Victorian coastal resort of Llanfairfechan. There are expansive views of the coastline on the way to the Drum where the main route divides, and in fine weather the hardy can take the high path and the less energetic the more sheltered lower route threading its way through Cwm Dulyn and Cwm Eigiau, where the desolate landscape is dotted with the abandoned and ruined dwellings of those who tried to make a living from the infertile soil. It is an eerie place, less populated now than at any time since the Bronze Age, with a quietness seldom experienced in the other hills of Snowdonia.

Best approached from Pen-y-Gwryd is Nant Gwynant, set in a much more gentle valley than the Llanberis Pass and the Ogwen Valley, and perhaps the most beautiful in Snowdonia, with Snowdon and Yr Aran in the west and Moel Siabod and the Moelwyns to the east. Here, some of the mountain-sides have a verdant mantle of broad-leaved trees intermingling with the evergreens, rather than an impenetrable jungle of conifers. The road winds downwards to Llyn Gwynant, and on to Llyn Dinas, where the bridge between the two lakes is the starting point of the Watkin Path, named after Sir Edward Watkin, who gave the path for public use, which ascends to Yr Wyddfa and on past Dinas Emrys where there is a group of

pre-Roman hut circles. The road then enters the alpine-style village of Beddgelert and the setting for another legend. Llywelyn the Great returned from hunting to find his faithful dog Gelert covered in blood and his baby son's cradle overturned. Llywelyn assumed that the dog had attacked and eaten his baby son, drew his sword and killed Gelert, only to discover that the dog had killed a wolf that had attempted to savage the child, and that the boy was unharmed under the cradle. *Bedd* is Welsh for grave and that, it is rumoured, is how the village got the name Beddgelert, although it is more likely that it actually originated from St Kelert who was associated with the Augustinian priory which once flourished in the area. Moreover, latter-day historians claim that the "legend" was the invention of one David Pritchard, the enterprising inn-keeper at the Goat Inn, who at the end of the 18th century decided to put Beddgelert on the tourist map. Nevertheless, a pleasant twenty-minute walk from the village along the riverside is "Gelert's Grave", supposedly erected by the repentant Llywelyn.

The glaciers did a thorough job on Nant Ffrancon, leaving a smooth and level profile, in contrast to the Pass of Llanberis.

Travelling out of Beddgelert one finds further facets of Snowdonia, to the north-west lies Rhyd-Ddu and one of the Snowdonia Forest Parks, and from this small quarrying village one of the gentler ascents to Yr Wyddfa can be made. Another path crosses the moorland and ascends to Y Garn before passing along a ridge to the summit of Mynydd Drws-y-Coed and Carnedd Goch. Further north lies Llyn Cwellyn, backed by the crags of Mynydd Mawr which, if approached from the opposite direction of Caernarfon resemble an elephant, and which some of the people of Waunfawr and Betws Garmon rather naturally call the Elephant Mountain. To the south is the picturesquely-wooded Aberglaslyn Pass, and the sparkling Afon Glaslyn has its source in Llyn Glaslyn high up in the shadow of Snowdon, from where it spills into Llyn Llydaw and on down the valley into Llyn Gwynant and Llyn Dinas, before flowing through Beddgelert on its way to Tremadog Bay.

The road travels south to Penrhyndeudraeth, a large quarrying village, where the philosopher Bertrand Russell spent the last years of his life in his country house on the outskirts of the village, and the region of Ardudwy is approached by a toll road leading south over the estuary towards Harlech. To the east is Maentwrog, one of the most picturesque villages in Wales, where the 7th century giant Twrog is said to have lived. The church contains the mortal remains of the Reverend Edmund Prys, a poet and archdeacon of the old Meirionnydd, who helped Bishop Morgan to translate the Bible into Welsh.

Llyn Dinas and Dinas Emrys. This sturdy dome of rock is associated with the legend of Merlin. Emrys is said to be a corruption of Ambrosius, considered to be Merlin's family name.

A few miles away is the Trawsfynydd Nuclear Power Station, built in the wild countryside which gave Hedd Wyn, a young shepherd who went to fight in the First World War, his poetic inspiration. Wyn was killed on the Somme, and in 1917, on one of the rare occasions when the National Eisteddfod was held outside Wales, the archdruid posthumously awarded

Llynnau Cregennan, a small haven of tranquillity encircled by dramatic mountain horizons.

him the black bardic chair which now stands in the farmhouse where he was born, and a bronze statue commemorating him stands in the main street of the village of Trawsfynydd.

There is open moorland to the east, and in the west across the moors lie the mountains Moel Ysgfarnogod, Rhinog Fawr, Rhinog Fach and Y Llether, which fill the skyline. These are commonly known as the Rhinogs, and stretch over twenty miles from Maentwrog to Barmouth. The terrain at the northern end of the complex has the reputation of being the toughest in Wales; the area is littered with boulders and scree from eroded gritstone slabs, with thigh-deep heather making progress both slow and treacherous. In the southwest of the area, beneath the rounded hills of Llawlech and Diffwys are Llyn Bodlyn and Llyn Irddyn and the barren, featureless and uninhabited Ysgethin valley. The aspect is bleak, and there is a ruined inn at the southern foot of Moelfre, where highwaymen robbed a party of gentlefolk on their way to attend a society wedding in Harlech. To the south of the valley is Pont Scethin, a small stone packhorse bridge on what was once the main highway between Harlech and London. A little way up the hill is the Janet Haigh Memorial Stone which reads *"Gogoniant i Dduw* – Glory to God – To the enduring memory of Janet Haigh, who even as late as her eighty-fourth year despite dim sight and stiffened joints still loved to walk this way from Tal-y-Bont to Penmaenpool . . . Courage traveller". The path continues above the western crags of Llawlech, and on through Bwlch y Rhiwgyr before its descent to the mouth of the breathtaking Mawddach estuary.

Here lies Barmouth, a popular sea-side resort which appealed to Wordsworth and Ruskin, both equally enamoured of the place. The quaintness of the little town only becomes evident away from the main street, up the steep alleyways and at Panorama Walk where the National

The reflected shades of rock and sky mingle and chase on the surface of Cregennan.

Trust acquired its first property *Dinas Oleu* – Fortress of Light, a modest four acres of clifftop donated by Mrs Fanny Talbot in 1895. In the late 15th century, Henry Tudor, then Earl of Richmond, landed on the quayside at the start of the campaign which ended with his defeat of Richard III at Bosworth Field, when he claimed the crown as Henry VII. Across the mouth of the estuary is a railway bridge and a footbridge constructed almost entirely of wood, but with a 400ft steel section in the middle which opened to give ocean-going yachts from Penmaenpool access to the open sea. The footway at the southern end of the bridge leads to the start of a footpath to the top of Cadair Idris.

Where the Mawddach estuary starts to widen to the west of Dolgellau is Garth Gell, the Royal Society for the Protection of Birds' nature reserve, and from the northern end of the small toll-bridge which leads to Penmaenpool there are marvellous views of the estuary's sands and saltings, with Cadair Idris to the south and the more distant Arans in the east. The charming town of Dolgellau has so many stories to tell that it is worthy of a book in its own right: three Roman roads meet here and coins bearing the name of Emperor Trajan have been unearthed; in 1404 Owain Glyndŵr assembled his last parliament in the town before signing his alliance with King Charles VI of France; Glyndŵr's cousin and enemy Howel Sele lived at Nannau, a mansion two miles outside the town, once the seat of the direct descendants of Cadwagan, son of Bleddyn Prince of Powys, and a Gorsedd Circle marks the site of an eisteddfod held at the town. During the 18th century it was a centre for the flannel trade; many of the farmers and cottagers had their own weaving looms; gold was mined in the nearby mountains and is still used to make the Royal wedding rings, and high in the hills above the town stands Bryn Mawr, former home of Rowland Ellis,

from which the famous Ladies College in Pennsylvania takes its name. After a visit by the first Quaker, George Fox, in 1657, many families converted to the faith, resulting in a concentration of Quaker houses and meeting places around the town, and Rowland Ellis was amongst the first of the Welsh Quakers to emigrate to America in 1682.

At Arthog, approached from the footbridge over the estuary or from Dolgellau, a footpath winds its way up the western foothills of Cadair Idris before levelling out on the shores of Llynnau Cregennan, two small lakes sandwiched between the cliffs of the northern face of Tyrrau Mawr and Bryn Brith. After passing between Craig-y-Llyn and Tyrrau Mawr the path divides, and to the left it ascends along Tyrrau Mawr to Penygadair, the summit of Cadair Idris. To the right it descends into the lush valley of Afon Cadair on its way down to Abergynolwyn. A bridge crosses the river at Pennant Farm, and a small detour leads to the ruins of Tyn-y-Ddol. Here stands a monument to Mary Jones, the girl who walked barefoot to the home of Thomas Charles at Bala to purchase a copy of the Bible, an act of faith which is reputed to have led to the founding of the British and Foreign Bible Society. Beyond Pennant Farm the path follows Afon Cadair's northern bank until it crosses a footbridge near Maes-y-Llan Farm and heads south to the ruined fortress of Castell y Bere, from where Prince Llywelyn-ap-Gruffydd – Llywelyn the Last – valiantly fought the armies of Edward I. Here in the Dysynni Valley stands the curiously shaped and appropriately named *Craig yr Aderyn* – Bird Rock, the only inland place in Britain where cormorants breed. From Castell y Bere the path briefly joins a narrow country lane to the west of Llanfihangel-y-Pennant before making its final descent into Abergynolwyn.

Corris awakes to a frosty December dawn.

Harlech Castle at one time stood with its feet in the sea, but several hundred years of geomorphology have conspired to leave Harlech high and dry. Deposits of sand and silt have built up almost a mile of coastal plain. Harlech from Mochras (left) and from Llandecwyn (right).

This large village developed as a result of the extensive slate quarrying at nearby Bryn Eglwys, and is a terminus for the Tall-y-llyn Railway which was originally built to convey the slates from the quarry to be exported by ship from Tywyn. The slate-carrying trains continued to run throughout the Second World War, but when the industry went into almost terminal decline in 1950 the line was closed, and would have disappeared for ever, if it were not for the preservation movements who have played a major role in saving and re-opening some of the narrow-gauge railways to passengers. The road leading out of the village to the south-west follows the same route as the railway to its other terminus at Tywyn, a resort on the shores of Cardigan Bay with the older part of the town being about a mile inland. The town has its origins in the 6th century when St Cadfan of Brittany established a church here on his pilgrimage to *Ynys Enlli* – Bardsey Island, which lies two miles off the end of the Llŷn Peninsula, and where the remains of 20,000 saints are reputedly buried.

Five miles to the south is Aberdovey, a pleasant resort with Victorian and Edwardian overtones, which marks the southern extremity of the Snowdonia National Park. This town was once one of the most important ports on the Cardigan Bay coast, and during the 16th century catered for Continental as well as coastal shipping. The port further expanded in the 19th century with the export trade in woollen cloth from Dolgellau and slates from Abergynolwyn and Corris. The town overlooks the Dovey estuary, with its fast flowing and dangerous currents, and at low tide, huge sandbanks. Eleven miles up river is Machynlleth, which lies just outside the Park border,

Llyn Tegid (Bala Lake).

40

with history going back to the Roman occupation when it was named *Maglona*. In Maengwyn Street is the site of Owain Glyndŵr's parliament of 1404, and it was here that he narrowly avoided being assassinated by his brother-in-law Dafydd Gam. In 1755 Machynlleth had a snuff industry, and in 1789 Titus Evans set up the first of town's seventeen printing houses. In the 19th century there were twenty-four inns, one of which was the Wynnstay Arms where George Borrow stayed during his epic journey through the Welsh countryside.

Heading north from Machynlleth the road hugs the edge of the Park and winds its way past two former slate-quarrying villages, with Corris deep in the valley of the Afon Dulas, and Corris Uchaf, where the local resource of slate has been used to build complete houses, walls and to fence fields. Further north is Tal-y-llyn, a beautiful lake which lies in almost unspoilt surroundings beneath the southern slopes of Cadair Idris. It is situated at the end of the Bala Fault, a deep, broad and almost straight valley, created by a geological tear-fault which caused the rock strata on one side to slip sideways. The long, shallow lake surrounded by reeded-banks is the source of the Afon Dysynni, which flows down to Abergynolwyn and on into Cardigan Bay.

It is all too easy, when sampling the delights of Cadair Idris and the Mawddach estuary, to overlook the coastal strip which stretches from Barmouth to Harlech Point: the region of Ardudwy. Sand dunes separate Dyffryn Ardudwy from the sea, and on the landward side the Rhinogs rise to over 2,000ft. Further north, the town of Harlech clings to the hillside and is characterised by granite houses and narrow streets which descend to the coastal plain. Here stands Harlech Castle, the only one of Edward's ring of massive castles within the borders of the Snowdonia National Park. It was

Slate waste encircles Blaenau Ffestiniog like a hastily erected barricade and hangs precariously above the rooftops.

43

built on the site of a Celtic fortress known as Twr Branwen, where Branwen of the White Neck, reputed to be one of the three most beautiful women in Wales, was claimed by the King of Ireland as his bride. The panoramic views of Tremadog and Cardigan bays and the surrounding mountains from the top of the castle's walls are spectacular, but somewhat intruded upon by the ubiquitous caravans and a modern housing estate on the coastal plain below. Across the marshes from Talsarnau is Traeth Bach, and on the northern shore of the Dwyryd estuary is the Italianate village of Portmeirion, created by architect Clough Williams-Ellis, and the setting for the cult television series, *The Prisoner*.

Tŷ Mawr.

North-east of Dolgellau lie the Arans, dominated by the twin summits of Aran Mawddwy and Aran Benllyn. The westerly slope which descends to the road between Dolgellau and Bala is boggy and uniformly dull in appearance, whereas to the east of the summits the terrain is precipitous with sharp crags, lavishly spattered with quartz. There is little public right of access here, and as a result, these remote hills are the most unspoilt in Snowdonia.

Bala, once the centre for the wool trade in North Wales when George III wore the famous stockings to relieve his rheumatism, lies at the north eastern end of Llyn Tegid, the largest natural expanse of water in Wales. In it lives the Gwyniad, a relic from the Ice Age, although not in the same league as the Loch Ness Monster. This rare fresh-water fish, unique to the waters of Llyn Tegid, is a member of the salmon family, and has recently been included on the list of protected wildlife in Britain. In the middle of the lake there is some turbulence where a definite current passes through it, which gives some credence to the claim that the River Dee passes through the lake without its waters mingling. The town's main claim to fame is as one of the leading centres of the Nonconformist movement in Wales in the latter half of the 18th century. Carmarthen-born Thomas Charles settled here and set up a chain of Sunday schools which, unlike their English counterparts, were attended by adults as well as children. The Sunday schools inspired a desire for learning amongst the people, and thousands of copies of the Bible, published in the Welsh language, were distributed in the area.

In the shadow of Arenig Fawr is Llyn Celyn, and beneath its waters is a submerged village. In the 1950s the hamlet of Capel Celyn stood on the banks of the Afon Tryweryn which runs down to the River Dee near Bala. It was in the middle of the site where the Corporation of Liverpool decided they wanted to build a reservoir to supply water to Merseyside. The Welsh local authorities were powerless to stop the scheme, and a whole community was dispossessed. At roadsides throughout this part of Wales the slogan *Cofiwch Dryweryn* – Remember Tryweryn, can still be seen painted on rocks and stone walls.

Morfa Harlech.

44

The River Conwy has its source in Llyn Conwy to the north-west of Arenig Fawr, from where it flows through part of the Migneint, one of the largest blanket bogs in Wales, to the village of Ysbyty Ifan. Originally a place of refuge and sanctuary in the care of the Knights Hospitallers of St John, it later became a base for pillaging thieves and murderers until they were ejected during the reign of Henry VII. Plas Iolyn, the residence of Elis Prys was situated nearby. Prys was commissioned by Cromwell to dissolve the Welsh monasteries, and was known as the "Red Doctor" as he habitually wore the red gown of a Doctor of Law. In Cwm Penmachno, which is virtually a cul-de-sac and ends with a cluster of disused slate quarry workings, is the village of Penmachno, where the church has a collection of 6th century Christian gravestones thought to be the oldest inscribed stones in Wales. In the largest of the Snowdonia Forest Parks is the beautiful and secluded Wybrnant Valley, and it was here in Tŷ Mawr, in 1545, that William Morgan was born. He was to become a Bishop and first translator of the Bible into the Welsh language. It was, of course, an achievement of considerable religious significance, but it also played an important part in the preservation of the Welsh language, which is still spoken by sixty-three per cent of the population of Gwynedd.

Moel Siabod seen from the hills between Llanrwst and Capel Curig is a graceful pyramid, but from Pen-y-Gwryd it is an almost shapeless boggy lump, and from the old quarrying village of Dolwyddelan, to the south east, it cannot be seen at all, as it is masked by low foothills. This is unfortunate, as it would have made a perfect backdrop to Castell Dolwyddelan, one of Llywelyn the Great's defences against marauding invaders, which stands proudly over the valley.

And finally, Blaenau Ffestiniog, an island in a sea of beauty which, in common with Bethesda at the northern end of the Ogwen Valley, and Llanberis at the bottom of the Llanberis Pass, was excluded from the Snowdonia National Park because of the irreparable industrial scars which had been inflicted, although they are all in the region of Snowdonia. Here slate dominates the whole town: the mountain-sides are scarred with the old workings; waste tips fill the sky-line, and slate has been used to build and roof the houses, to build walls and make fences, for garden paths – even in death there is no escape from slate, as most of the gravestones are made of it. The town bears witness to the ravages of unfettered industrial development, and stands as a grim reminder for future generations.

Anyone who has made a journey through Snowdonia must feel something of the forces that pull at the hearts of the expatriate Welsh, which make them want to travel home to attend their major tribal gatherings, the Royal National Eisteddfod and the Royal Welsh Show at Builth Wells, and perhaps understand a little of what is meant by *hiraeth*; not mawkish homesickness, but a yearning to be part of the fabric of the country.

The high crags of Cadair Idris, etched by the warm light of the setting sun.

Harmoni

Silk stepping, willing worker – on the hill
  and in far off places;
See with what skill in that distant cwm
His flock is sent into the fold.

Thomas Richards

The idyll of the Welsh pastoral and sheep-rearing way of life is a fiction, although many look back nostalgically to "the good old days", and every generation has had writers eulogising about the past with its timeless agricultural rhythms. If there ever was an idyll, it was the preserve of the rich and privileged, and not the farm-worker. For centuries, the life of farm-workers in Wales was one of medieval penury: they lived at subsistence level in hovels which they often shared with livestock and worked an average of seventy hours a week for meagre rewards.

Few buildings survive to demonstrate the organisation of early medieval farmsteads, and in much of Wales the patterns of communal cultivation which did exist broke down early, as the tradition of sub-dividing land holdings between sons restricted the development of large economical units. However, single large farms were established on the higher, and initially less attractive, mountain-sides, and in the 19th century, some of the miners and quarrymen had a goat, a pig and other livestock, together with pasture on which to graze them. Their stone cottages and holdings spread over the hillsides around the quarries and their lives settled into a basic working pattern. The animals and land were usually tended during the week by the women, while the men stayed in the barracks and dormitories at the slate quarries and mines, walking home at the weekends to be with their families, and to make their contribution to the husbandry of their holdings.

Sheep-farming practices changed little for generations and were relatively unaffected by the agricultural revolution of the late 18th and early 19th centuries. The old patterns and lifestyle, which had provided the inspiration for some of the most moving prose and poetry written in both the Welsh and English languages, started to change immediately prior to the Second World War, and the dying way of life has been well documented by Thomas Firbank in his best-selling book *I Bought a Mountain*, published in 1940. In it he graphically describes his purchase of Dyffryn Mymbyr, a sheep farm set into the hillside above the road between Capel Curig and Pen-y-Gwryd, and his subsequent battle for economic survival in the hostile environment.

Pont Aber-Geirw.

The way of life has changed more in the last forty years than it did in the previous two centuries, and although shepherds can still be seen wearing peaked-caps, and with their macintoshes tied at the waist with string, the modern sheep farmer is just as likely to be seen riding a motorbike across the hills, with his dogs in a basket strapped to the pillion.

The sheep no longer have to be walked to market along the drovers' roads, a task which was the source for ancient legends and folk-lore, and the farmers' lives are made easier by lorries, Land-Rovers, tractors, electric shearing clippers and all the other paraphernalia of modern farming. They now have electricity and bathrooms, and many have become part of the revolution in information technology, and spend some of their time in their "electronic cottages" hunched over word processors, grappling with accountancy software packages and spreadsheets. On the surface much has changed, but the struggle to work in harmony with nature, which can be harsh and predatory as well as benign, continues.

In autumn, when tourists dwindle to a trickle of determined climbers and hill-walkers, the cycle of the sheep-farming year begins. The flock is rounded up and brought down from the mountain grazing and crucial decisions about re-stocking the flock have to be made. The farmer carefully selects the best of the existing ewe lambs, and buys new rams at the October sales to avoid the problems caused by inbreeding. The ewe has a five-month gestation period and comes into season every seventeen days, and most will have been served within the first three weeks of being put with the ram, timed so that lambing will coincide with the growth of the spring grass, to

Harmony. Nantmor (above, left). Pearl bordered fritillary on ragged robin (right).

50

Pant Glas.

provide the milking ewe with an ample supply of food. At the first mating the ram's belly is painted with an oily red ochre which marks the ewe's rump when she has been served. The colour is then changed, so that the ewes who are going to lamb at a later stage can be identified. On the lower slopes in Snowdonia, after the sheep have been counted, the ewes and rams are taken back up to their grazing grounds, where they will spend the winter together. At the same time, the ewes from the higher grazings are brought down to more accessible areas so that the ram can serve them. The yearlings are moved down off the mountain grazings to the lowland pastures, to fatten them up and prepare them for the harshness of their succeeding years on the mountains.

With the onset of winter, storms start to ravage the higher peaks, and any ewes that were missed in the earlier gatherings are forced down by the bad weather to lower grazings, when their summer fleeces have to be removed. With the lower temperatures it is important to leave some of the fleece for protection, and modern technology gives way to the old practice of using hand shears. It is now that the mountain ewe comes into her own as a survivor in the harsh environment where she has to live and search for grazing, and the shepherds must be constantly alert to the rapidly changing weather patterns. Sheep sense the onset of bad weather, and the shepherd must move them out of sheltered hollows onto the more exposed mountain-side, so that they are not buried in drifting snow. If the weather becomes too severe, the sheep are forced to lower ground in search of food, and their hunger can drive them to eat poisonous vegetation such as rhododendrons, which can kill them.

Ensuring that the flock has enough to eat is the farmer's main concern throughout the harsh winter and the unpredictable early spring as lambing

Bryn-pig.

approaches. Traditionally, little supplementary feed was given, except when the snow was too heavy on the ground to permit normal grazing, when the sheep would be given a little hay. Every farmer has his own views on the subject of feeding; some prefer hay, which is relatively easy to transport over the hills; others prefer silage, or cereal blocks, especially when lambing is approaching and the ewes need extra nutrition and others swear by liquid feed.

With the coming of March, the farmer's life becomes more varied as he attends to the farm's maintenance, injects the ewes to protect them from disease, and doses them for worms. It is also time for dealing with bureaucracy, so out come the calculators and word processors, and a concerted attack is made on the mounting paperwork of grant applications, VAT receipts and Income Tax Returns.

Now is also the time when, in years past, the Snowdonia farmer and his family would leave the *hendref* – winter dwelling, and move up into the hills to spend the lambing season and summer months in their *hafod* – summer dwelling. The summer dwellings which survive today are usually holiday cottages, or the homes of people who earn their livings in the towns, with the others as derelict, crumbling reminders of a former life-pattern and tradition.

For the sheep farmer, April is by far the busiest time of the year. Lambing gets under way in earnest, and it is a time for constant vigilance when he and his dogs patrol the farm in an almost endless cycle of midwifery. It is a testing time for both the man and his dogs, and a stern test of their stamina and initiative, as well as their knowledge of the habits and instincts of the lambing ewes. It is also a time when the predators get to work. Twin lambs are particularly prone to attack by foxes, as the ewe cannot watch

Llanfachreth. Like churches or stone circles, dry-stone walls and old barns become cherished landscape features, physical evidence of our long association with the land and generations past.

both her offspring at the same time, and crows are another danger. The average mortality rate on a hill farm at lambing time is ten per cent, and another problem for the farmer is the orphan lambs, who must quickly be found surrogate mothers. When a ewe has lost a lamb she naturally becomes a potential adoptive mother. The farmer works quickly to skin the dead lamb, and then wraps the skin around the foster lamb, so that to the ewe it smells like her own. After a couple of days the ewe smells her milk on the new lamb and accepts it as her own.

In May, lambing continues at a less frenetic pace, and it is time for the farmer to inspect the dry-stone boundary walls before the sheep are sent back onto the mountain for summer grazing. Some of the walls will have been damaged by the frost and rain, and others by the sheep jumping over them to reach different grazing. Most of the boundary walls are over five feet in height, with the foundations being an average three foot wide, tapering to a width of about a foot at the top. Building and repairing the walls is an art, and another test of the shepherd's versatility. Within six weeks of birth the lambs are gathered for counting and ear-marking, when they must also be dosed to prevent worms and other internal parasites, and at the same time the ewes' tails must be docked as a precaution against infestation.

As the season progresses, the sheep are moved progressively up to higher grazing to leave the home fields free for the growing of hay and silage, and where the high mountain grazing is unfenced, it is considered necessary to get the ewes and their lambs on the mountain by May, so that the young ewe lamb can become familiar with the farm's grazing boundaries at her mother's side. The word *cynefin* is much used by the shepherds and hill farmers in Snowdonia, and this is the word's most common usage,

referring to the Welsh sheep's inherited knowledge of its own territory, beyond which it will not stray. However, motorists travelling through Snowdonia and suddenly confronted by stray sheep in the middle of the road, may have a sceptical attitude to the concept.

On the lower farms shearing begins in June, and on the higher properties in July, and on many of the hill farms in Snowdonia the process follows the old traditions, and is the biggest social and communal event in the sheep-farming year, when neighbouring farmers get together to shear up to eight hundred sheep a day. At first light, the men and dogs are up on the mountain tops, rounding up the sheep and then herding them down to the shearing area. In the early morning the sheep are constantly moved around to dry off the dew on their fleeces, and then herded into pens for sorting. Stray sheep from neighbouring farms will have got in with the main flock, and these are penned separately so that their owners can collect them at the end of the day.

Communal shearing is not as widespread as it used to be, and today the old tradition is gradually being replaced by gangs of itinerant shearers who work their way from farm to farm, with the local men helping with catching and handling the sheep.

When the sheep have been shorn, they are dipped and then marked with an initialled iron stamp which has been coated in a coloured marking fluid, to identify which farm they belong to. Each fleece weighs about three pounds, and the wool is used in blanket and carpet making, and although a fleece is only worth about a pound, the sale of seven or eight hundred of them is a valuable source of income.

Rather than trying to master nature, traditional hill-farming methods work in harmony with the seasons and the natural cycle of the land.

The unsullied upper reaches of the Afon Dyfi. Cattle, sheep, woodsmoke and wellies.

Many of the hill-farmers have to face the problems of the imbalance between the amounts of grass available in the summer and winter; the fact that much of the land on the mountains has been overgrazed, and that often there is not enough grazing to support large flocks. One solution has been the acquisition of additional land on the coastal plains, which is run in conjunction with the hill farm. One family of hill farmers in Cwm Prysor, to the east of Trawsfynydd, spend many hours on the road travelling to and from a holding just outside Aberdaron at the far end of the Llŷn Peninsula, but consider it a small price to pay for the availability of better grass late in the season to fatten their stock. For others, however, the solution isn't that simple. In 1986, the nuclear disaster at Chernobyl covered the hills of Snowdonia with radioactive fall-out, and the movement of sheep on one thousand four hundred holdings was restricted, and had to be checked and cleared by the Ministry of Agriculture, Fisheries and Food. At the beginning of 1993, nearly four hundred holdings were still subject to regulations restricting the movement of sheep.

In late summer the lambs are weaned off the ewes so that they come into season at the right time the following year. They are put to graze on the new growth springing up on the mown fields, some to be fattened for slaughter, and others to be retained as flock replacements, and they are given three separate vaccinations to immunise them against a variety of diseases. After weaning, the ewes are sent back to grazing high up on the mountains, and the ram lambs are usually slaughtered before they are eight months old.

As the light fades and the evening air cools, sea mists roll up from the valley below and gradually obscure the slopes of Craig-las.

In September, the sheep are dipped to prevent scab, checked for signs of footrot, and the ewes are dosed to protect them against fluke. It also the time for the 'draft' sale, when around half a million Welsh mountain ewes

59

Otter populations are declining in Snowdonia. Forced out by pollution, disturbance and habitat loss, they act as a barometer to the state of the environment as a whole.

Stonework mellows and blends so that eventually, it hardly seems to be the work of man. The living walls, Hafod-y-porth (left), Coed Bwlch-derw (above right).

are sold to lowland farmers. They are an attractive buy because of their low price, mothering ability and capability for producing good quality milk in sufficient quantity, as well as needing a minimum amount of shepherding. It is an important sale where presentation counts, and there is much last-minute grooming to show the ewes at their best, but it is also an important social occasion, when old friends meet to catch up on all the news and gossip.

The sheep, who has given man work and an income, fed him and clothed him, shares its habitat with a variety of wildlife in the constant battle for survival. Three hundred years ago there were golden eagles in

61

Snowdonia, but today the larger birds of prey are the peregrine and buzzard. The peregrine, however, suffered a serious decline in numbers in the 1960s caused by the use of certain highly toxic agricultural pesticides. These have now been banned and the peregrine is starting to re-establish itself in ever increasing numbers. The raven has also survived persecution and is much in evidence, and there are kestrels, short-eared owls and barn owls. In the west of the area, in the summer months, the chough nests in and around the old quarries and mines. Where there are spreads of heather on the moors the odd red grouse can be seen, but they generally prefer the drier climate on the more easterly moorlands. In the spring there are meadow pipits and skylarks on the rushy moorlands: wheatears on the scree; wrens on the high rocks; teal and mallard breed on the upland bogs, and there are a few noisy communities of black-headed gulls to disturb the peace and tranquillity.

Around the coast there are great seabird colonies of guillemots, razorbills, kittiwakes, herring gulls, cormorants, shags and fulmars, and along the estuaries are herons, gulls, grebes, geese, ducks and waders. In what is left of the native woodlands there are woodpeckers, finches, tits, thrushes, redstarts, wood warblers, pied flycatchers, tree creepers, nuthatches, jays and buzzards. Here too, are polecats, badgers, grey squirrels, bank voles, hedgehogs, woodmice, shrews, dormice and bats. There is little wildlife in the jungles of conifers that seem to march relentlessly over the hill-sides, but the pine marten, a rare member of the weasel family, survives in the plantations, as does the sparrowhawk.

Mammals, sheep apart, are a rare sight on the mountains, although there are foxes, and the nocturnal stoats and polecats. By far the commonest is the field vole, an important link in the food chain, and the prey of all the predators. More easily seen, although usually in the distance, are the herds of goat, which are mistakenly thought of as being wild, but are the descendants of the large numbers of domestic goats that were kept on the hill-sides, and have since become feral.

The mountains, moorlands and peat bogs of Snowdonia are acidic places whose vegetation consists of rough grassland, heather, bracken and too many rhododendrons. However, there is some plant-life, including sedges, sundew, clubmosses, the lesser twayblade orchid, and the bog orchid. Up in the lime-rich crags there is holly fern, purple saxifrage, alpine mouse ear, hoary whitlow-grass, mountain avens, moss campion and the celebrated Snowdon lily.

Although not idyllic, sheep farming is a good way of life with fine traditions, and the shepherds of Snowdonia have a motto which they share with farming communities the world over: "Live life as if you would die tomorrow, farm as if you will live for ever." A concept which is becoming increasingly difficult for them to live by, as their life of hard-won harmony is under threat from influences which are beyond their control.

Pen-y-bedw.

Bygythiad

I was here before, when heart
and mind and eye were one,
when knowledge, and unease
fled before serenity.
Here peace no longer dwells,
between looking and death.

Dinah Griffiths.

Many of the ancient nations of the world have among their myths, legends and folklore a hero who, when the nation is confronted with mortal danger, will awaken his slumbering legions and come to the rescue. Down the centuries the Welsh remembered the story of Arthur's sleeping knights, and there must have been many times when they have fervently wished that King Arthur would awaken his knights in the hidden cave high on Lliwedd's precipices, and rescue them from the marauding armies who threatened their existence. Today, the threats facing Snowdonia and its people are of a more pervasive kind, not easy to confront or deal with effectively, and Arthur's services are probably more desperately needed now than they have ever been.

Soon after the Snowdonia National Park had been designated in 1951, problems started to arise. The ideals of the Standing Committee, who had worked so hard to introduce the National Parks and Access to the Countryside Act, became increasingly difficult to attain, and their basic precept that "There is not a square mile too much of wilder country, and there is urgent need of a national policy for conserving the whole" was in serious danger of being ignored. The county councils of Caernarfonshire, Denbighshire and Meirionethshire, to whom the Park authorities were responsible, jealously guarded their planning and other powers, and the Park authority was little more than a county council committee.

The late 1950s and early 1960s saw the birth of consumerism as we know it today, and Harold Macmillan, who was Prime Minister during some of the boom years coined the phrase "You've never had it so good", which epitomised the mood of the times. The new prosperity created a huge increase in demand for consumer durables and the electric power to run them, and for the first time motor cars were within the purchasing power of ordinary people.

In Snowdonia the Central Electricity Generating Board played its part in attempting to satisfy the increasing demands of industry and the new

Rhaeadr-y-cwm.

65

Trawsfynydd Nuclear Power Station. According to National Parks and Access to the Countryside Act, the national parks were established ". . . for the purpose of preserving and enhancing their natural beauty . . ."

consumers, but with little regard for the needs and wishes of the local inhabitants or for the spirit, concept and aims of the National Park. It was apparently blind to those grim reminders of earlier industrial damage; the irreparable scars of the slate mines and quarries of Bethesda, Llanberis and Blaenau Ffestiniog.

Over the years the landscape and the people of Snowdonia have paid a heavy price for the generation of electric power for both industrial and domestic consumption. In the early 1920s, the Dolgarrog Hydroelectric Scheme was devised to supply power to the aluminium works at Dolgarrog on the western side of the Conwy Valley. The scheme was designed to utilise the energy available from the water-courses that flow down the Carneddau range of mountains, and involved enlarging Llyn Cowlyd and

Porthmadog and Moel-y-Gest.

66

Llyn Crafnant sits in secluded isolation at the road's end, a mountain cul-de-sac of peace and tranquillity.

constructing a new reservoir, Llyn Eigiau. Disaster struck soon after the project was completed. The pressure of Eigiau's waters built up, bursting through the dam, which had been built on insecure ground, and flooding the wide upper valley. The raging waters were channelled into the bottleneck of the Dolgarrog Gorge, gouging huge two hundred ton boulders from the mountain-side, destroying a terrace of cottages in their path, and flooding into an electrically-fired furnace at the aluminium works causing violent explosions. Sixteen lives were lost. Large boulders still lie in the village as a macabre reminder of that dreadful night. The aluminium works were closed, but the power station continues to operate as part of a re-designed scheme, and by 1957 four generators were operating, supplying electricity for public consumption. A few miles away, pylons now march their way relentlessly across the northern edge of the Carneddau, and at Traeth Bach in the region of Ardudwy they cross the beautiful Dwyryd estuary and the surrounding area, as part of the National Grid carrying energy to distant conurbations.

In the early 1960s, an early Magnox type nuclear power station was built at Trawsfynydd, and was the only nuclear power station to be built within a National Park. It was shut down for safety reasons early in 1991, and despite negotiations with the Nuclear Installations Inspectorate, Nuclear Electric were ordered to close the station in 1993. It has been estimated that it will take at least one hundred and thirty five years to restore the site to its original green field condition.

The mountain railway winds its way up Snowdon's north-western flank, and the pipeline of the Cwm Dyli Hydroelectric Scheme winds its way down the south-eastern flank. When it was first planned, although it was to use renewable energy resources and would be clean to operate, objectors wanted the proposed twin pipelines to be buried underground so

In the cool evening light, Dinas Emrys seems imbued with an air of mystery and timelessness.

The sturdy peak of Yr Eifl and its companions Gurn Goch and Gurn Ddu crowd the northern shore of the Llŷn Peninsula, whose island-like airiness offers a different, more subtle beauty than its brooding neighbour.

that, after the construction work had been completed, there would be the minimum amount of damage to the visual environment. They were presented with the argument that to put the pipelines underground would create more lasting damage to the environment than running them overground, and that the pipelines would soon be covered with foliage. What had been overlooked was the rapacious appetite of sheep, who eat almost everything in their path. One pipeline, three feet in diameter, that channels the water down the mountain-side from Llyn Llydaw to the power station on the floor of the valley has recently been painted green. The area immediately surrounding it remains as barren as on the day the construction work was completed.

In the early 1970s, construction work started on the Dinorwig Pumped Storage Electric Scheme in the mountains high above Llanberis. When the scheme was first proposed, there was an enormous amount of controversy about the potential damage to the landscape, which was expected to add to the scars already inflicted by the slate workings over a century earlier. Some damage was done, but part of the system is hidden inside the mountain Elidir Fawr; the high reservoir Llyn Marchlyn Mawr blends with its surroundings, and the cables carrying away the generated electricity are buried underground. There was some detrimental effect on Llyn Peris, the scheme's lower reservoir, and some new buildings were erected, but they are so dominated by the slate galleries that their impact to the casual observer is minimal. The Prince of Wales described the enterprise as "a triumph of commonsense, reasonableness and sheer technical expertise", giving rise to a faint stirring of hope in the hearts of those who strive to protect Snowdonia's environment.

Copper mining on the slopes above Nant Gwynant has left its scars, but nature heals in time and the ruins of a lost industry slowly blend into the landscape.

The Welsh Water Authority have also been responsible for environmental damage, and in the western Carneddau, with a complete disregard for any landscape considerations, built a tarmacadamed road leading from the Ogwen Valley straight up to the Ffynnon Llugwy reservoir. Similar harm was done by building an access track across the northern Carneddau to Llyn Anafon, when Bronze Age relics were destroyed. Moreover, the track has since attracted some irresponsible owners of four-wheel-drive vehicles, who are causing further damage to the land and disturbing the peace of the area. The destruction caused such a furore that consultative procedures were agreed between the Welsh Water Authority, the Snowdonia National Park Authority and Gwynedd Archaeological Trust before any work would be allowed to begin in environmentally and archaeologically sensitive areas in the future.

The consultative procedures were, however, ignored when the Welsh Water Authority decided to install a pressure relief tank close to Pont Scethin on the southern end of the Rhinog Hills near Barmouth. The whole area is a designated Ancient Landscape, where there is a presumption against any development which will affect the environment in any way, and is one of the most sensitive and fragile localities in the whole of Snowdonia, and perhaps the most important archaeological area in the whole of Wales. The sub-contractors moved in with their JCBs, and the caterpillar tracks of the earth-moving machinery crushed their way across the old drovers' tracks, and the ancient London to Harlech road. Concrete was mixed on the first stones of Pont Scethin, the ancient pack-horse bridge, and a hundred yards away the tank with its pipes and stopcocks was partly buried in a large hole. The area was strewn with alien aggregate, and a quagmire, in places fifty

yards across and swimming in diesel oil, scarred the green moorland. Where the tank stood proud, the surface of the moor was scraped into a mound to cover it, and left as barren soil.

The Forestry Commission has also played its part in the despoliation of the landscape with dark, sterile plantations of conifers which have spread over the moors and mountain-sides. Just as damaging is the contribution the coniferous afforestation makes to increasing the acidity of the area. The trees trap acid rain from the atmosphere, the spate floods caused by the plantations' deep drainage systems pollute water courses, and the soils release aluminium salts, killing fish and other wildlife.

It comes as a shock to many visitors to learn that acid rain is having a detrimental effect on Snowdonia, where there is little industry, and few obvious signs of atmospheric pollution. However, the broadleaved trees are displaying similar symptoms of damage to those in Europe, where acid rain has been blamed for the wide-spread deaths of millions of trees, though there is some controversy as to whether the unhealthiness of the trees here is actually caused by acid rain. Although the prevailing wind in the area is south-westerly, easterly winds blowing from the industrial heartlands of England can bring acid rain. Seventy-five per cent of the sulphur dioxide in the rain comes from industry, and it is four times as acidic as "normal" rain. The problem is exacerbated by the granite rocks that make up most of Snowdonia's mountains. They are very hard rocks when compared to chalk and limestone, and do not have the same characteristics to neutralise the acids in rain. The high rainfall in the area and a hard geology results in acidic run-off into the streams, rivers and lakes. Recent research into lake sediments has revealed that the process has been going on since the start of the industrial revolution, and we are now suffering from a pollution build-up that started over two hundred years ago. The acidity of the soil is confirmed by the continually spreading presence of self-seeding rhododendrons, leaving little scope for native flora to grow under the shade of their beautiful foliage.

In April 1986, the "impossible" explosion occured at Chernobyl in what was then the USSR, spewing its deadly radioactive cocktail hundreds of miles into the atmosphere. The fall-out covered Snowdonia, adding to the naturally occuring emissions of radon, a carcinogenic gas, from the granite rocks. Seven years later, the radioactive caesium is still in the soil, and the sheep on nearly four hundred holdings have a higher than normal level of caesium in their bodies, and cannot be sold directly to the market. The sheep testing procedures, and the restrictions of movement placed upon them, will continue for at least another generation.

In 1974 the Government introduced a reform of local government, and as part of the process the counties of Caernarfonshire, Meirionethshire and part of Denbighshire were dissolved and re-organised to become Gwynedd

Vale of Ffestiniog.

73

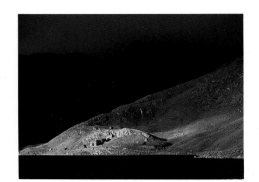

Cwm Dyli and Llyn Llidaw, haunt of peregrines, playground of light and shadow.

County Council. The Snowdonia National Park Authority operates within the county council structure, with the council providing twenty-five per cent of the Park's funding, and the other seventy-five per cent being provided by the Countryside Council for Wales. It also receives additional revenue from grants, and generates some of its own income. National Park Authorities have two principal duties; to protect and enhance the natural beauty of the Parks, and to ensure that the public has the access to enjoy them. In Gwynedd there is an additional emphasis on the well-being of local communities, and the Snowdonia National Park Committee has defined its aims as follows: "To preserve and enhance the natural beauty of the National Park, to strengthen the social and economic well-being of the communities within its boundaries and to promote its enjoyment by the public".

The Snowdonia National Park Authority is now a more powerful organisation with wider responsibilities than in the early 1950s, and is empowered to formulate policies and programmes to do with Park matters without the approval of the county council. It rarely becomes involved in the direct lobbying of central Government, but in 1987 it considered that the threat to the area created by pollution was so great that it issued its "Acid Rain in Snowdonia" statement. This stressed that strong representations to Government "should be made to hasten the reduction of pollutants that cause acid rain deposition", urging them to act to reduce emissions from power stations and cars, although the long term benefits of such action would not be felt for many years.

Pollution created by the burning of fossil fuels is, of course, not a modern phenomenon, the first air pollution law was introduced in the reign of Edward I, and in 1306 a Royal Proclamation banned the burning of coal in the city of London. The first recorded offender was beheaded for the crime of polluting the air. Today, attempts to resolve the problem are rather more restrained, and the UK Government is committed to reducing sulphur dioxide emissions from power stations by sixty per cent by the year 2003. However, they are not requiring power stations to install expensive pollution filtering equipment, but encouraging them to burn coal with a lower sulphur content. It is unlikely that such a policy will achieve the ninety per cent reduction in sulphur dioxide emissions that the Department of Environment admits is needed to restore the acidified lakes to anything like their natural condition.

Nature thwarted. Channels funnel water destined for the Afon Llugwy into Llyn Cowlyd Reservoir.

In November 1989, the Countryside Commission set up a Panel, under the Chairmanship of Professor Ron Edwards, to undertake a thorough review of the National Parks in England and Wales, and the Panel's report was published in March 1991. The report was wide-ranging, comprehensive and addressed itself to the unique problems facing the Snowdonia National Park Authority. In September 1991, the Minister of State for Wales, Sir Wyn Roberts, told the annual conference of National Park Authorities that the Government had decided to accept the recommendations of the National

Afon Glaslyn and Dinas Emrys.

Llandecwyn Chapel.

Parks Review Panel that all National Parks should become Independent Authorities within the Local Government framework, although no time-scale was given for the introduction of legislation. However, the Government has confirmed its intention to reorganize local Government in Wales on the 1st of April 1995. The Park Authority is pressing for its own legislation to become law before then, otherwise it could be faced with answering to two separate local authorities, with further upheaval when its own legislation becomes law.

The Snowdonia National Park only owns about one per cent of the Park, mainly picnic sites and car parks, which makes it difficult for them to honour their statutory obligation to provide public access, and many members of the public are confused as to who actually owns the Park. The use of the words "National" and "Park" suggests to many visitors that the whole area is owned by the nation, and that they therefore have freedom of access to every part of it. The largest area is, in fact, owned by farmers and private individuals, and provides little or no right of public access, though some 50,000 acres, approximately nine per cent of the total area, is owned by the National Trust who encourage the public to visit all of their land. The National Trust and National Park authorities believe, rightly, that respect for the environment cannot be engendered by denying access to it, and the National Park runs educational walks for visitors, and provides facilities for outdoor pursuits organisations and for universities and schools who come here to study the environment, together with residential Professional Training Courses for countryside staff. The National Trust has recently employed a Countryside Education Officer who is funded by some of the money already raised by the National Trust Snowdonia Appeal.

Tourism, which can inflict serious damage on the environment, employs nearly ten per cent of the workforce, and in generating an income of nearly £1.3 billion for the whole of Wales, has now replaced sheep farming as the main industry in North Wales. But the pressures it creates on the under-funded infrastructure of Snowdonia are enormous. The ever growing numbers of tourists can unwittingly disturb wildlife and the grazing patterns of sheep, and contribute to the increasing erosion of the land. Snowdon itself, with half a million visitors a year reaching its summit, is literally wearing out, and Moel Siabod and Cadair Idris are suffering similar problems. In addition to the ordinary wear and tear caused by the ramblers and walkers, fell running is becoming increasingly popular and accelerating erosion, and the use of mountain bikes is destroying footpaths at an alarming rate. Motorcycles and four-wheel-drive vehicles when indiscriminately driven over the hills create an enormous amount of damage. The behaviour of those few who drop litter everywhere, destroy the tops of walls by using the stones to throw at sheep, and rip up stones from footpaths to make a splash in streams, makes the increasing reluctance of farmers and other private landowners to make more of their land available for public use easier to understand.

One of the biggest stories in the North Wales media in recent years has been the upgrading of the A55 Expressway, which has had the positive effect of relieving the traffic pressures in the medieval town of Conwy, but has also contributed to the increase in the numbers of tourists who visit the area in their cars, with the exhaust emissions adding to the pollution. In an attempt to ease the traffic pressure the Park Authority subsidises a special Snowdon Sherpa Bus park and ride scheme, and buses run from Llandudno via Betws y Coed, Porthmadog, Caernarfon and Bangor, and will stop on

The beauty of water left to its natural course.

80

request at any safe stopping place in the National Park. The service also provides a round-the-mountain route allowing walkers to climb Snowdon by one path, descend by another, and catch the bus back to their starting point.

Over the years, the social and cultural composition of Snowdonia has been dramatically altered by the increase in rural unemployment and the decline in public services in the villages. The green-field sites, shopping malls and supermarkets which are springing up along the new expressway are a serious threat to the continuing economic well-being of shops in the small communities, thereby placing additional strains on the social structure of the area.

The present Government's extensive road building plans will add to the demand for aggregates, and already eyes are already turning towards Snowdonia and its resources. Plans for the extension of existing quarries have been mooted, and there have been suggestions that the mountains of slate waste could be utilised for road building. If the quarrying operations are extended to cope with the increase in demand, further despoliation of the fragile landscape will naturally follow, and with the decline of the railway system in the area, the already strained road network will become clogged with large lorries transporting the aggregates to distant road construction sites. If the slate waste is utilised, the pressure on the infrastructure would also be enormous, although it could be argued that once the waste had been removed, the land could eventually be landscaped in an attempt to restore it to its pre-industrial rural condition.

The threat to the existence of farming communities increases, and the numbers working in the uplands continues to decrease and seventy-five per cent of full-time jobs have disappeared in the last few years. Increasingly,

Llandanwg Beach at low tide provides rich pickings for waders, curlews and oystercatchers. Nearby Morfa Harlech and Morfa Dyffryn offer secluded nesting grounds and in spring, they are spangled with a mass of wild flowers.

farmers on small upland farms can no longer afford to continue, and their properties are being bought by larger neighbouring farms or absentee farmers to extend their grazing. The empty farmhouses either become holiday cottages to supplement the farmers' incomes, or are sold to people who have no connection with the land, thereby contributing to the social breakdown of rural Welsh-speaking communities. Thirty years ago it was inconceivable that the thriving coal mining valleys of South Wales would be devoid of pits, and become the Industrial Heritage Museums that they are today. Yet if drastic action is not taken to put the economy of the sheep farming communities of North Wales on a secure footing, the farms of Snowdonia could become no more than Agricultural Heritage Museums, with those who are still employed to tend the remaining sheep displaying their skills for tourists.

The relentless search for energy resources continues, and exploration for oil and gas is currently taking place in the northern part of Cardigan Bay, where some of the exploration blocks are adjacent to the Snowdonia and Heritage Coasts of Gwynedd. The Braer disaster in January 1993, which resulted in crude oil contaminating the seas off Shetland, highlighted the threats posed by oil transportation, and a similar spillage into Cardigan Bay, the habitat of rare bottle-nosed dolphins, could breach the Berne Convention on the Conservation of European Wildlife and Natural Habitats. Many environmentalists and conservationists argue that the exploitation of any energy resources should be excluded from National Parks, even those that rely upon renewable resources such as harnessing wind and wave-power, solar energy and generation of electricity with tidal flows. Although they would not pollute the atmosphere they could damage the visual environment, and tidal schemes would require the damming of estuaries, destroying birds' wading and breeding grounds.

Since the beginning of the 18th century Snowdonia has been damaged by man's ignorance, greed and the exploitation of its natural resources, and its people have suffered, not only from the harshness of nature, but from the ills inflicted by industrialisation and commerce. The task now, is not to create an idealised countryside, frozen in a time-warp and protected from any form of innovation, but to bring all the demands made upon the countryside into harmony, with a commitment to avoid the pitfalls of cosmetic conservation and to create genuine sustainability within the local economy. This is not a nostalgic wish for a mythic golden age, but the need for a concerted effort by all of those involved to resolve the problems which have been inherited from previous generations, and to confront the current threats.

This then, might prevent the dreams of those whose efforts led to the establishment of National Parks from turning into a nightmare.

Pont Croesor. The rain at last abates, but too late to save the day.

Dymuniad

Give me peat and a mountain ash,
Its round apples in garlands above.
The flames of its leaves igniting a secret fire,
And the sun of my homeland lingering in the sky.

Nesta Wyn Jones.

In the mid-nineteenth century attempts were made to enclose large areas of Hampstead Heath and Wimbledon Common in London, public outcry at which led to the formation of the Commons Preservation Society in 1865. The Society instituted legal proceedings to defend the rights of commoners and the interests of the public, who also enjoyed access to the Heath and Common. Robert Hunter, a young lawyer, was engaged to collect evidence, and at the age of twenty-four he was appointed as the Society's solicitor.

Octavia Hill, a social reformer, joined the Committee of the Commons Preservation Society in the early 1870s. She wanted to provide open spaces of any kind for the benefit of those who lived in the overcrowded London slums. Her sister Miranda had founded the Kyrle Society whose aim was to bring beauty into the lives of the poor, and Octavia formed the Kyrle Society's Open Spaces Committee, with Robert Hunter as its Chairman. They converted old and derelict graveyards into peaceful gardens; small areas of land ripe for development were turned into play grounds; in Lincoln's Inn the gardens of the lawyers' inner sanctum were opened for public use, and some of the more enlightened local authorities were persuaded to support larger schemes.

However, the difficulties encountered in his charitable work prompted Robert Hunter to propose the creation of a statutory body which would be endowed with wide-ranging powers to acquire land and buildings, to be preserved and held in trust for the benefit and enjoyment of the general public. In 1895, the National Trust for Places of Historic Interest or Natural Beauty was registered by Robert Hunter, Octavia Hill and Canon Hardwicke Rawnsley under the Companies Act as a public company not trading for profit, with the powers to acquire and preserve beautiful and historic places. Their first property was donated by a friend of Octavia Hill.

In 1907, the Trust was incorporated by an Act of Parliament which established it as a statutory body. Its mandate included, so far as practicable, the preservation of the natural aspects of the land, its features and the animal and plant life, together with the provision for the Trust to maintain its buildings and land for purposes of public recreation, resort or instruction. A crucial provision of the Act gave the Trust its unique power to declare its

A wintery sky over Glyder Fach.

Tryfan and the Ogwen Valley.

property "inalienable" so that it can never be sold or mortgaged.

By 1923 the Trust owned one hundred and two properties, and in 1928 it established a publicity committee to create more public awareness of its aims and activities, resulting in a trebling of the membership.

From then on the Trust grew steadily, and money from legacies, gifts and public subscription enabled it to secure large stretches of the coastline and countryside, as well as a number of ancient buildings. By the mid-1930s, it became clear that the survival of many of Britain's stately homes and country houses, with their contents and surrounding estates, was threatened by heavy taxation and death duties. This led to the establishment of the "Country Houses Scheme" under which, a house – with or without its contents – may be presented to the Trust with a financial endowment to maintain it in perpetuity. The aim is to preserve houses not as museums but as homes, preferably lived in by the families traditionally connected with them.

In 1965, when it already protected one hundred and eighty-seven miles of coastline, the Trust launched its Enterprise Neptune appeal. Some £15 million pounds has since been raised, and five hundred and thirty-four miles of Britain's coast are now safe from damaging development, and access to it is permanently available to the public.

In 1967 the Benson Report suggested that efforts should be made to extend the opening times of the Trust's properties and land, and that more amenities, such as car parks and picnic sites, should be provided for the public's convenience and enjoyment. With some of its historic houses it is difficult for the Trust to extend the opening times, as agreements made with donors placed irrevocable restrictions on the times that public access to the properties would be available. Moreover, in common with the Snowdonia

Glyder Fach. The summit plateaux of the Glyderau is an incredible place, a barren moonscape, strewn with natural sculptures. Castell y Gwynt hangs precariously over Cwm Bochlwyd.

Cwm Bual and Foel Goch.

Llyn Idwal.

National Park Authority, the Trust faces the dilemma of the conflicting demands of preservation and public access; visitor pressure is contributing to the erosion of the buildings and land, and does much to destroy the atmosphere of the places where they seek enjoyment.

Although, as with the National Parks, its name suggests that it is owned by the nation and run by the State, the Trust is independent, and depends on the generosity of those who give it properties and the money to maintain them, as well as over two million subscribing members and other friends and supporters, and is "national" in the sense that it works on behalf of the public with the supportive recognition of successive Governments.

The day-to-day administration of the Trust is carried out by its executive staff at the Head Office, and at its regional offices in England, Wales and Northern Ireland. There is an independent National Trust for Scotland. Policy is determined by the Trust's Council, half of whom are nominated by institutions such as the British Museum, the Ramblers' Association and the Royal Horticultural Society, with the other half elected by the Trust members at their Annual General Meeting. The Council appoints an Executive Committee which in turn appoints the Finance Committee and a Properties Committee and regional committees around Britain. The committee members have specialist knowledge relating to the Trust's work, and give their time and services free of any charge.

Today, the Trust is the largest private landowner in Britain, and in North Wales it owns and administers some impressive properties which include Penrhyn Castle, Plas Newydd, Bodnant Garden, Chirk Castle and Erddig, a complete and unaltered 17th century Country House. In Snowdonia

it owns Tŷ Mawr, the birthplace of Bishop William Morgan, who translated the Bible into the Welsh language. The house has recently been restored from a modernised dwelling to its probable 16th–17th century appearance, and stands in the beautiful and secluded Wybrnant Valley near Betws y Coed.

Buildings apart, the Trust's most priceless treasure is its open countryside, and here in Snowdonia its mission is clear. It is to acquire and preserve "areas of outstanding natural beauty or historic interest", and the Trust believes that the ultimate protection can only be achieved by its ownership and caring stewardship. Thus the Trust can save areas of outstanding landscape for the benefit of the nation, and in so doing, can guarantee "space to breathe" for all people – for all time.

Snowdonia is unique in Europe with an extraordinary diversity of habitat contained within such a small area: the majestic mountains, some with steep cliffs and jagged precipices and others with gently rounded

The wind-scoured and snow-flurried crags and screes of Cwm Idwal provide a habitat where relic communities of Arctic plants and Alpine flowers maintain a precarious foothold, survivors from the last Ice Age. Moss Campion (top left). Polytrichum Moss (bottom left). Mountain Avens (right).

contours; extensive upland heaths with peat moors and boglands, glacial lakes, deciduous woodlands, riverside meadows and undulating green valleys. Over the years the mounting threats to the area have been pervasive, seemingly imperceptible, but they interact with each other, and gather momentum. Pollution, acid rain, global warming and the after-effects of the nuclear disaster at Chernobyl are taking their toll, but so too are the more localised problems of over-intensive modern agricultural practices, the decline in upland farming, lack of regeneration in the deciduous woodlands, tourism pressures, and the increase in the provision of leisure activities, many of which are totally unsuited to the local environment.

Snowdon Lily. In latin – Lloydia serotina, *after the Welsh botanist Edward Lloyd, who discovered it here in the 17th century.*

The Countryside Council for Wales, created out of the amalgamation of the Nature Conservancy Council and the Countryside Commission, has the task of formulating the overall strategy for the conservation of the area and injecting funds to aid remedial tactics wherever possible. Their main concern is with the problems of close-cropped vegetation caused by the combination of overgrazing with the ever-increasing pressures of recreation which denude the mountains of their protective layers of soil, a problem exacerbated by the harsh winter weather conditions. They have also been concerned with the economic problems facing the farmers on the smaller farms, which are unable to support large families, leading to the younger members of the family drifting away in the hope of finding more lucrative employment in large towns. This leaves fewer shepherds to tend the sheep and regulate the grazing patterns, so the sheep eat the best pasture, leaving the hills resembling moth-eaten blankets. The Countryside Council now pay farmers to rotate the grazing by keeping sheep off parts of the mountains at certain times of the year, and provides incentives to encourage farmers to keep hay fields which are more labour-intensive, and which are the natural habitat of flora and fauna, in an attempt to restore the ecological balance. The Council have also introduced a scheme called *Tir Cymen* – Good Husbandry, which will give farmers annual payments for lower stock ratios together with capital grants for repairs and the restoration of traditional buildings and walls.

The Snowdonia National Park Society, which has its headquarters at *Tŷ Hyll* – Ugly House, situated on the road mid-way between Betws y Coed and Capel Curig, is a registered charity whose aims are to seek a balance between the needs of residents with the interests of visitors; to act as a watch-dog in an attempt to prevent inappropriate schemes being implemented for commercial expediency, and to promote what they consider to be worthwhile initiatives. The Society has recently launched the Snowdonia Park Society Farming and Landscape Award. The objectives of the biennial competition, which is open to the occupiers of around 1,500 holdings within the National Park, are wide-ranging, and in addition to the quality of the general farming, the judges will look for positive conservation work having

The walls and deeper recesses of the Devil's Kitchen are festooned with mosses, ferns and a rich variety of Alpine flowers. Safe from even the most daring mountain goat.

94

been carried out as part of good environmental practice for the whole farm. Attempts to safeguard stone walls, slate fences, hedgerows, earthbanks, wildlife areas and the weatherproofing of traditional stone buildings will be taken into consideration. Other criteria include the organised control of rubbish, the conservation of deciduous woodlands and the maintenance of new plantings, the care of water courses and wetlands and the positive management of rough grazing, grassland and unimproved coastal land.

The ubiquitous Rhododendron ponticum, first introduced into Britain from Turkey, Spain and Portugal in the middle of the 18th century, found its way into Snowdonia from the estates of wealthy landowners and now covers almost thirty square miles of the Park. It is a menace that threatens the area's indigenous animal and plant life by releasing toxins from its roots which smother plant growth in its shade and poisons animals. Poisons and burning have been used in attempts to eradicate it, and the National Trust cleared a large area at Aberglaslyn with the help of an Employment Action Team of workers. After using the mountains for training exercises the British Army joined in the battle, sending in units to burn and clear several square miles of the beautiful aliens.

Y Garn broods beneath angry clouds, embroiled in a storm of its own making.

The National Trust is the largest private landowner in the Snowdonia National Park, owning and caring for 50,000 acres. Its holdings include 18,000 acres of the Carneddau and Glyder mountain ranges to the north and south of the Ogwen Valley, and the peaks of Carnedd Dafydd, Carnedd Llywelyn, Pen yr Ole Wen and those of Y Garn, Tryfan, Glyder Fach, and Glyder Fawr together with the Cwm Idwal complex. Around the village of Beddgelert the Trust cares for 2,000 acres on the Aberglaslyn and at Cwm Bychan, where the land ranges from riverside meadows to the heather-clad hills of Nantmor on the east of the magnificent Aberglaslyn Pass – known in the past as *Y Gymwynas* – The Favour. Further south, near Dolgellau, lie some 1,800 acres around Dolmelynllyn, where the land falls from the dramatic peak of Y Llethr in the Rhinog mountain range to the softer, greener woodlands of the Mawddach valley, and on the eastern flank of Y Llethr the Afon Gamlan winds its way down to the *Rhaeadr Du* – Black Waterfall, near Ganllwyd on the Dolgellau to Trawsfynydd road. To the south of Betws y Coed the Trust cares for the 20,000 acres of the Ysbyty Estate, including the Migneint blanket bog.

Such a large and varied landscape requires not only complex management, but constant vigilance, and at the end of the 1980s the Trust conducted a series of surveys which revealed that much of the fabric of their holdings in Snowdonia is under serious threat. There are six independent summits above the 3,000ft level on the main ridge of the Carneddau and a seventh, Yr Elen, just over half a mile to the north-west of Carnedd Llywelyn. On a clear day the views are spectacular with Colwyn Bay to the north, and the Glyders with the Snowdon massif to the south. The National Trust

Glyder Fach. Sun chases shadow and cloud harries sunlight.

Llyn Idwal. With Castell-y-Geifr hanging like a bastion from the shoulder of Y Garn.

boundary runs for almost the total length of the summit ridge line, from Drum in the north almost to Carnedd Dafydd in the south-west. The approach to the ridge by way of the Aber Falls, along Afon Goch, and then from Carnedd Uchaf to Foel Grach showed little sign of wear and tear. The main ridge almost to Carnedd Dafydd in the south is heavily used, but it is a broad ridge with gentle inclines, and has been able to sustain its level of use with little serious damage. However, the total length of the path line was clearly under stress and there were places where erosion was clearly beginning to show itself.

Along the ridge to Carnedd Llywelyn there are junctions and outlying spurs giving access to and from the ridge, and from Carnedd Dafydd over Pen yr Ole Wen the descent to the south-west is exceedingly steep from the summit down to the car park and Ogwen Cottage on the valley floor. It is here that the most serious erosion of the whole Carneddau main ridge exists. The descent from the summit begins easily enough, over steep, but

Cwm Idwal, where ice has sculptured a masterpiece of natural form.

96

Mountain Goats, agile foragers, high above the Pass of Llanberis.

Nant Ffrancon. The mountains bequeathed by the last Ice Age are but shadows of their former selves, spoils left behind in the wake of the glaciers.

grassy, terraces and shelves, and the path is forced into distinct rocky ridges which offer the only way down. Here the descent becomes very steep and in one or two places demands scrambling skills, and the worst of the erosion is at the bottom where the path descends 350 yards over a horizontal distance of only 500 yards. The damage can be seen quite clearly from all parts of the traverse on the Glyders across the valley, and if it is allowed to worsen, it will cause serious and very unsightly erosion.

Cwm Idwal is the home of the rare Snowdon Lily and is a nature reserve with a rich variety of species. It is also one of the most spectacular high mountain basins to be found anywhere in Britain, and its rock and mountain topography is of such classic proportions that, with the close proximity of one of the major through-roads of the area, it is a major tourist attraction. It appeals not only to those who wish to reach the higher summits, but those attracted by the drama of its scenery, and who want to experience a real mountain atmosphere without the physical effort normally associated with such experiences. The classical geography of its layout with the lake dramatically overshadowed by high mountain, crag and spur, pinnacled ridge, hanging valley, buttress, waterfall, gulley and ravine, its magnificent wild tangle of huge boulders below *Twll Du* – Black Hole, commonly known as the Devil's Kitchen, make this one of the most important areas for educational visits by students of all ages and levels of scholarship. The ease of access to Llyn Idwal from the road at Ogwen Cottage, together with pressure from visitors staying at the nearby youth hostel, and the fact that nature trails encourage ever more people to visit, is reflected in the serious degree of erosion in the area.

Llyn Idwal and Twll Du.

The whole area falls within the limits of a Site of Special Scientific Interest, and over the years a great deal of remedial work to the footpaths has been carried out by the Trust. Generally the technique used in path building has been the use of steps, some of which are of massive proportions, and an enormous amount of physical effort has obviously been put into the work, which starts near the exit from the visitor car park and follows the lines of the right-of-way almost to Twll Du itself, where nearly two miles of the path has been completely rebuilt.

Snowdonia splendid on every scale. From the close detail of a woodland waterfall to the broad brush canvas of a summer mountainside. Rhaeadr Du (top right), Drws y coed (bottom right).

The tracks to the summits of Glyder Fach, Glyder Fawr and Y Garn are straightforward, heavily used mountain paths which have received no remedial work. The descent of the north ridge of Y Garn has none of the

Nant Gwynant.

severe erosion and damage of the other paths in the area, with the exception of the scree slope which is vulnerable to the damaging and thoughtless pastime of scree-running. The descent of Bristly Ridge is a rock climb with little signs of wear, although the alternative and easier path to the east of the ridge is badly damaged, and the path down from Tryfan is one of the most seriously eroded in the whole area, particularly in the steep section west of, and adjacent to, Nant Bochlwyd.

The footpath surveys were just part of a complete review of the National Trust's 50,000 acres in the whole of Snowdonia, and highlighted the problems in the Carneddau mountain range, the Glyders and the 20,000 acres of the Ysbyty estate where there are over fifty farms, many under 100 acres in size. Here, the partnership between the Trust and the local farming communities

Nant Ffrancon.

protects much of this upland area from decay, with reduced rents offered to tenant farmers as an incentive for proper husbandry and the preservation of traditional buildings. The surveys revealed the need for a total additional expenditure of £5 million, and although the Trust receives grants from other statutory bodies such as the Snowdonia National Park Authority, Cadw Welsh Historic Monuments and the Countryside Council for Wales, they were faced with a shortfall of £2 million. Following the success of Enterprise Neptune, the decision was made in 1990 to launch the National Trust Snowdonia Appeal under the presidency of actor Anthony Hopkins, in the hope of raising £2 million by 1995.

The funds raised will be spent on desperately needed remedial work and a variety of projects to conserve and enhance the local environment.

Llyn Idwal and Pen yr Ole Wen.

One of the major tasks will be undertaken by footpath teams, who will tackle the restoration of the most severely eroded paths around Cwm Idwal and Tryfan, where up to fifteen miles of path needs urgent attention. The task is not only labour-intensive, demanding considerable stamina and perseverance, but on the section of the ascent to Llyn Bochlwyd where torrential winter rain has scoured the footpaths to form deep gullies, technical knowledge and skill is also needed. Here, the ancient "pitched stone" method, often described as a horizontal wall, will be used. The technique was used by monks in the Lake District over three hundred years ago, and involves the use of specially constructed water gullies, angled at a precise angle of 52 degrees to the flow, to break the velocity of the water. The whole area then has to be re-seeded with a "boot resistant" grass. In the same area, close to

The bulk of Pen yr Ole Wen (top right) and the great dragon-back of Tryfan (bottom right) face each other across the Ogwen Valley.

104

106

Water spills from the rocky cup of Cwm Idwal (left) and early snow dusts the whaleback Pen Llithrig-y-Wrach (right).

Tryfan, an area of grassland will be fenced and native trees planted, to form a screen around the campsite on Gwern Gof Isaf Farm, in the spectacular Ogwen Valley. The screen will provide the campsite with shelter from the harsh winds, and help to disguise an eyesore which spoils the panoramic views. This project is part-funded by the Countryside Council for Wales.

During the last few years the Trust has been gradually extending the stone wall which runs from Ogwen Cottage beside Llyn Ogwen, and insetting gates and stiles to provide proper access to the mountain footpaths. Up to now, the work has been done by an Employment Training team, and was of such high quality that the Trust received a Prince of Wales' Award for the project. However, with the Government cuts in Employment Training provisions, additional work on the wall will be carried out by local countryside contractors, many of whom were trained on the original project, placing an extra strain on the Trust's financial resources.

On the Ysbyty estate, the field systems are essentially 18th century in character although many of the walls and dykes belong to the medieval period. But with incomes rarely above £5,000 a year, the upland farms on the estate can barely support the families working them, let alone the numbers of yesteryear, who were needed for the labour-intensive tasks of dry-stone wall building and hedgerow repair. Funds raised by the appeal will provide cost-effective assistance in the form of seed money, which will enable the farmers to obtain additional grants for the preservation and repair of these valuable landscape features. Thus local people will act as contractors to the Trust, caring for their own environment, but it is a slow and costly business, and a highly-skilled dry-stone wall builder can only repair up to seven yards of wall in a day. To make any real impact on the problem will take

Llyn Cwmffynnon and Glyder Fawr.

several years, and hundreds of tons of rock will have to be moved, lifted and placed precisely by hand.

Biological Site Management, a rather grand name for the maintenance of traditional hay meadows, needs to be undertaken at Aberglaslyn, where modern agricultural methods would have destroyed the wildlife-rich meadows long ago. Here, through carefully controlled grazing, hay mowing at precise times and with the surveillance and control of water levels, colonies of wild orchids and butterflies can be protected.

The mixed agricultural and woodland estate at Dolmelynllyn near Dolgellau which fell into disrepair during the last century needs reinstating. Extensive new fencing and repairs to dry-stone walls and hedgerows are badly needed, and the existing woodland needs protecting from overgrazing, to allow natural regeneration to take place. New tree plantings of natural species must be carried out, which is a very long term process. Once planted, the young saplings may need up to ten years of constant care and protection, and the woodlands will need positive long-term management if they are to survive for their full life-span of four hundred years.

The programme and projects which have been costed and planned for the next half decade, represent only the minimum essential work to stabilise the situation, and prevent the further dereliction of walls, paths, traditional buildings and the irretrievable loss of wildlife habitat. To turn the tide of environmental degradation will take not only innovative and skilful management, but hard work and money. It will also need the support of private individuals from all sectors of the community, organisations and charitable institutions, the business world, and central Government.

The task is enormous, and should not be underestimated, but the natural threats diminish when compared to those created by man's foolhardiness. When Thomas Telford was given the job of building the road which was to become the A5, he was told to proceed "without regard to special interests", an attitude sadly still in evidence today. The majority of industrialists and politicians of all parties have thought only of exploiting the natural resources available, with no thought that the earth, our only resource, must pay the heavy price. In Wales we face a decline in the use of our language, the disappearance of regional traditions, local lore, skills, customs, entertainments and initiatives, and an ancient culture has been almost irretrievably lost.

In September 1987, the National Park Festival was held at Chatsworth House in Derbyshire, which is a fine example of environmental care and enlightened estate management. The President of the Council for National Parks, Mr Brian Redhead, made a speech with the theme "Not ours, but ours to look after", which epitomised the sentiments of those who have striven so hard to bring about the designation of the National Parks and the formation of the National Trust. It also epitomises the feelings of those who now wish to preserve these treasures for the benefit of future generations.

Tryfan casts a long shadow across Llyn Ogwen and the lower slopes of Pen yr Ole Wen, gripped by frosts that last all through the day.

Bibliography

Beach, Russell	*Touring Guide to Wales*, AA/Hutchinson.
Bogle, James	*Artists in Snowdonia*, y Lolfa.
Borrow, George	*Wild Wales*, Collins.
Bowen, Keith	*Snowdon Shepherd*, Pavilion.
Firbank, Thomas	*I Bought a Mountain*, Harrap.
Fishlock, Trevor	*Talking of Wales*, Cassell.
Fishlock, Trevor	*Wales and the Welsh*, Cassell.
Gillham, John	*Snowdonia to the Gower*, Diadem.
Godwin, Fay & Toulson, Shirley	*The Drovers' Roads of Wales*, Wildwood House.
Gwynn, Richard	*Way of the Sea. The Use and Abuse of the Oceans*, Green Books.
Havord, Bryn	*North Wales Lifestyle*, The North Wales Weekly News Group.
Minhinnick, Robert	*The Environment of Wales*, Seren Books.
Monkhouse, Patrick	*On Foot in North Wales*, Diadem.
Morris, Jan	*The Matter of Wales*, OUP.
Morris, Jan	*Wales. The First Place*, Aurum Press.
Ordnance Survey	*Leisure Guide: Snowdonia and North Wales*, AA/Ordnance Survey.
Perrin, Jim	*On and Off the Rocks*, Gollancz.
Perrin, Jim	*Yes, To Dance. Essays from Outside the Stockade*, The Oxford Illustrated Press.
Pye-Smith, Charlie & Hall, Chris	*The Countryside We Want*, Green Books.
Redhead, Brian	*The National Parks of England and Wales*, The Oxford Illustrated Press.
Rees, Ioan Bowen	*The Mountains of Wales*, University of Wales Press.

Also, the publications of the Snowdonia National Park Authority, the Snowdonia National Park Society, the National Trust, Gwynedd County Council, Cadw Welsh Historic Monuments, Greenpeace, Nuclear Electric and The Friends of the Earth – Wales.

Acknowledgements

The publishers would like to extend their thanks to Laurie Gardner of the National Trust Snowdonia Appeal for all his support and enthusiasm for this book.

Graham Nobles

I'd like to express my thanks to my friends at the National Trust, in particular, the Estate Wardens Richard Neale and Mark Donnelly and Field Biologist Derek Hughes for all their help and advice; Hywell Roberts, C.C.W Warden for Cwm Idwal; the staff and management of the Welsh Mountain Zoo, Colwyn Bay; and finally, my wife Les and son Gavin, for their enduring patience.

Bryn Havord

In researching and writing this text I have become heavily indebted to friends, colleagues and many others, all of whom have been generous with their time and commendably patient in answering all my questions. In particular Jim Perrin; mountaineer, author and conservationist, who gave me access to his own research material; Robert Minhinnick of Friends of The Earth Cymru who gave me so much of his non-renewable energy resource: time, and Dr Rod Gritten the Snowdonia National Park Ecologist who, as always, willingly shared his knowledge and experience.

My thanks also to Alan Jones, John Ellis Roberts MBE and Glenys Edwards at the Snowdonia National Park Authority. Laurie Gardner, Neil Allinson, Richard Neale, Elfyn Jones, Janet Harley and especially Victoria Thomas at the National Trust. Martyn Evans at the Snowdonia National Park Society, Keith Jones of the National Farmers' Union: Wales. Linda Simmonds at the Welsh Office, Vaughan Johnson of Cadw Welsh Historic Monuments, John Roberts at Gwynedd County Council, Mick Felton at Seren Books, John Saven at Greenpeace and Tracy Williams of Nuclear Electric. I thank Ioan Bowen Rees, author and former Chief Executive of Gwynedd County Council and Margaret Wyles for sharing with me some of their extensive knowledge of Welsh poetry, William Condry, Johanna Firbank and Ken Russell-Jones.

I am, of course, also indebted to Anthony Hopkins and finally my wife Elaine, for her support and many helpful suggestions, as well as her usual pertinent criticisms.

Become a National Trust Friend of Snowdonia

Working with the environment, in partnership with the communities and people who live and work on the land, is a long-term affair. This is the positive action coming generations will thank us for.

The future of this landscape, its mountain fortresses, oak woodlands and wildlife, its unique culture and language, lies in our hands. Together we can help preserve the beauty of this place for centuries to come. Snowdonia can be saved.

When you make a donation or covenant, you become a National Trust Friend of Snowdonia and are eligible for special benefits. These include a newsletter on the progress of the appeal and the Trust work in Snowdonia, a free Friend's car sticker and guided tours of the area with a Warden. These and other opportunities are exclusively for those individuals who have helped to make this vital work possible.

Please join me in this contract with the future. Help us today, so our memories of this special place can remain a reality – forever.

If you can help us to save Snowdonia's rare beauty and tranquillity, please write to me for more information, or make a donation, care of:

Sir Anthony Hopkins, President of the Appeal
The National Trust Snowdonia Appeal
The National Trust, Trinity Square, Llandudno, Gwynedd, LL30 2DE

The National Trust is a registered charity number 205846

Follow the Country Code

When you visit Snowdonia please respect not only the environment,
but those who live and work there.
* Guard against all risk of fire. Fasten all gates.
* Keep your dogs under close control.
* Keep to public footpaths across farmland.
* Use gates and stiles to cross fences, hedges and walls.
* Leave livestock, crops and machinery alone.
* Take your litter home with you.
* Help to keep all water clean.
* Protect wildlife, plants and trees.
* Take special care on country roads.
* Make no unnecessary noise.

Don't let the weather catch you out!

The changeable weather in Snowdonia is notorious. If you are a walker, especially on the higher ground, your day could be ruined by the sudden change in the weather. In the winter and spring there could be serious consequences if you are not properly clothed and don't take sensible precautions. Mountaincall Snowdonia, which operates in conjunction with the National Park, gives the local forecast plus information on ground conditions, followed by a national 3–5 days general forecast. Ring Mountaincall on 0839 500 449. Calls cost 36p per minute cheap rate and 48p per minute at all other times. It could not only save your own life, but the life of a member of a Mountain Rescue Team, who all give their services, often in dangerous circumstances, free of charge.